Teaching Reading as a Language Experience

Teaching Reading as a Language Experience

second edition

MaryAnne Hall

Georgia State University

Charles E. Merrill Publishing Company
A Bell & Howell Company
Columbus, Ohio

Published by
Charles E. Merrill Publishing Company
A Bell & Howell Company
Columbus, Ohio 43216

This book was set in Caledonia and Radiant Medium.
The Production Editor was Lynn Walcoff.
The cover was designed by Will Chenoweth.

Library of Congress Catalog Card Number: 75-16897

International Standard Book Number: 0-675-08666-3

3 4 5 6—80 79 78

Printed in the United States of America

Contents

v

Preface

The purpose of this book as stated in the preface to the first edition was "to describe this approach and to identify instructional practices which can be followed in teaching reading in the language experience approach." That purpose remains as the central focus in this second edition. The major difference between the editions is the expansion of the theoretical foundations of language experience communication and the extension of instructional suggestions. The section on prereading has been expanded so as to give greater attention to language experience activities prior to beginning reading.

The additions to this second edition have stemmed from extensive contact with children and teachers in schools throughout the country. Again and again, the same questions would occur among a group of teachers trying language experience techniques for the first time. One common reaction is what this writer calls the doubting one—"Can an idea so seemingly simple be trusted in the implementation of a reading program?" The writer is reminded of Eric Hoffer's statement, "It is not at all simple to understand the simple."[1] Another reaction is that of "It sounds like too much work." To that this writer's response is that for those who are willing—as good teachers are—there are different ways of expending effort in teaching reading. "Too much work" may be related to "I'm not sure how to do it." Another reaction of teachers is "It makes so much sense." Of course, these perceptive teachers are the ones that save a consultant's day! Hopefully, in practice, the sensible grasp of what constitutes effective reading instruction can be combined with a knowledge of how to implement language experience reading programs.

As noted in the preface to the first edition, the book is *not* a collection of practices for teaching. However, ideas for teaching are presented as illustrations of the language experience approach in action. This book *is* a description of the theoretical base of the language experience approach and the implementation of this theoretical base in a classroom setting. The practical ideas included are to illustrate the basic philosophy of

---

[1]Eric Hoffer, *The Passionate State of Mind* (New York: Harper and Row, Publishers, 1955, 1968), p. 125.

fostering communication in a creative, personal, and functional way of learning and teaching.

This writer believes that communication skills can best be developed in an integrated and functional framework of teaching reading and language skills. Integrating reading instruction with the other language arts has long been a goal of reading programs, and the language experience approach truly illustrates this goal through all classroom reading experiences. Another belief of this writer is that teachers should recognize the linguistic nature of the reading process and adapt instructional practices for teaching reading with an emphasis on communication.

The book is organized in two parts. The first two chapters establish the theoretical background of the language experience approach and its relationship to the total elementary reading and language curriculum. The last seven chapters are concerned with the practical implementation of the language experience approach in the classroom. These chapters discuss experience stories, creative writing, vocabulary development, and literature experiences as well as the teaching of specific prereading and reading skills. The final chapter summarizes the information presented and describes an effective setting for the language experience approach.

While this book is devoted exclusively to language experience reading, the reader should not assume that this approach is advocated by the author as the only means for teaching reading or that this approach is without limitations. Informed teachers will utilize practices from a variety of approaches. This source can add to the background of the elementary teacher who wishes to draw upon the language experience framework as one component in a total reading program.

Special thanks go to the many teachers and teacher education students who tried and revised some of the procedures described here. Their comments greatly clarified the activities.

Special thanks also are due Ray Stanford for the photographs, Mildred Jones for making the arrangements for the photographs at Roswell Elementary School in Fulton County, Georgia, Martha Scott for typing, and Lynn Walcoff for her thorough editing and maintenance of the production schedule.

Teaching Reading as a Language Experience

chapter one

The Nature of the Language Experience Approach

The essence of the language experience approach is the use of the language and thinking of the learner as a foundation for reading instruction. Each learner's language and personal experiences are used to create reading materials which help to show the reader the relationship between written language and his already familiar oral language. This chapter expands upon the preceding explanation and explores the linguistic and psychological foundations of this approach.

A Description of the Language Experience Approach

The cornerstones of language experience learning are language and experience and the interrelatedness of the two. Loban comments on the importance of these learning components, "Through experience and through language we learn. Experience needs language to give it form. Language needs experience to give it content."[1] The form and content of language experience reading programs are the language and experiences of the learner, and the form and content will therefore differ from child to child and from group to group.

---

[1]Walter Loban, "What Language Reveals," in *Language and Meaning*, ed. James B. Macdonald and Robert R. Leeper (Washington, D.C.: Association for Supervision and Curriculum Development, 1966), p. 73.

1

Sylvia Ashton-Warner has written movingly of the power of language experience learning in *Teacher.*[2] In a recent book, *Spearpoint,* she expresses the heart of language experience: "The professional formula—Release the native imagery of our child and use it for working material—remains timeless, changeless and axiomatic, but the application of it needs constant variation."[3]

The language experience approach for teaching reading is based on the interrelatedness of language and reading with the experience of the learner as the core from which language communication radiates. Language experience reading is viewed as a communication process closely related to communication in speaking, listening, and writing. The language experience approach uses children's oral language and experiences for the creation of personal reading materials. This approach to reading integrates the teaching of reading with the other language arts as children listen, speak, write, and read about their personal experiences and ideas. A child's speech determines the *language patterns* of the reading materials, and his experiences determine the *content.* The language experience approach is based on the concept that reading has the most meaning to a pupil when the materials being read are expressed in his language and are rooted in his experiences.

As children see their spoken thoughts put into written form they can understand the nature of communication in reading in addition to recognizing words. Communication is stressed as children speak, see the speech represented by printed symbols, and then read the written representation of their speech. The association of meaning with the print is built into the reading of the personally created materials of the language experience approach.

The sequence of communication in the language experience approach can be represented by diagram 1.

DIAGRAM 1

The Communication Sequence in the Language Experience Approach

Step 1—Speech	Step 2—Recording	Step 3—Reading
The child expresses his thoughts.	The child or the teacher writes the child's thoughts.	The child reads the written record.

Communication
of meaning

---

[2]Sylvia Ashton-Warner, *Teacher* (New York: Simon and Schuster, Inc., 1963).
[3]Sylvia Ashton-Warner, *Spearpoint* (New York: Alfred A. Knopf, 1972), p. 17.

In the language experience approach, the purpose of communication underlies the three stages of producing reading materials depicted in diagram 1, which shows the child's involvement as he moves from talking to recording to the reading of his thoughts. As the child sees his speech encoded into the printed symbols, the communication of the meaning of his speech in written form is evident to him. As he decodes the printed symbols and associates them with his previously spoken thoughts, he is communicating through reading.

Reading is not "talk written down" but instead is the process of decoding and comprehending printed symbols. In the language experience approach, the written record itself may be viewed as "talk written down," but the reading of the written record involves decoding the printed symbols and responding to them with meaningful interpretation.

CHARACTERISTICS OF THE LANGUAGE EXPERIENCE APPROACH

The characteristics of the language experience approach were implied in the preceding description, but for purposes of emphasis, three major characteristics are elaborated below.

Pupil-composed materials constitute a major source of reading materials in the language experience approach.   Reading materials are developed as children talk about their ideas and experiences; their talk is recorded and the written record is then used for reading. In initial reading instruction, group and individual experience stories are used for reading instruction instead of published reading materials. Although pupil-produced materials are of prime importance, other materials also are utilized since children need to develop skill in reading and obtaining meaning from many types of materials. As children advance, supplementary reading of selections from basal readers, trade books, newspapers, content area texts, and other materials is included in a well-rounded reading program. Chapters 3–9 devote considerable attention to the various types of and procedures for using pupil-developed reading materials.

The interrelationship of all the communication skills is stressed.   Reading is not taught apart from but is dependent upon the other facets of the language arts. Reading is a language activity, and the ability to communicate through language is essential for success in reading. The four facets of the language arts can be classified as either receptive or expressive. Listening and reading are receptive, while speaking and writing are expressive. In the language experience approach, children's listening, speaking, and writing skills are incorporated with reading instruction. As children increase their listening and speaking facility, they increase their ability to understand ideas encountered in their reading.

There are no vocabulary controls in the reading materials other than the extent of a child's speaking vocabulary.   The initial reading material is not limited to a few simple words or to short, artificial sentence patterns with a planned amount of repetition. There is, however, the inescapable repetition of frequently used words. In recording the pupil's speech, the teacher should *not* shorten or alter sentences in an attempt to control vocabulary. In the language experience approach when a pupil reads content which he has first spoken, the teacher is certain that the words and syntactical patterns employed in reading are in his spoken language. Ways of developing both speaking and reading vocabularies are discussed in chapter 5.

ATTRIBUTES OF THE LANGUAGE EXPERIENCE APPROACH

Definitions and characteristics provide one means of describing the language experience approach. However, teachers who work with this approach need a greater understanding of the philosophical framework or the distinctive attributes than that supplied by the definition and explanation given for the characteristics. The language experience approach is a personal, communicative, creative, and purposeful way of learning and teaching.

The language experience approach is a personal *way of learning and teaching.* Language experience reading starts with and values the reader—his thoughts, his experiences, his language, his products, his uniqueness. The language experience rationale and the application of the approach can be appropriate for many, but in each case the person makes the language experience materials unique. Language experience reading is free and unstandardized. The learner in the language experience approach is actively involved in the reading process as he creates and shares his reading. In the language experience approach it is possible to have material of high personal interest to each child. Group writing experiences are encouraged, but since the content of group stories will be related to common experiences and group interests, these materials will also be personal to the group members.

All teachers are confronted daily with the problem of creating an instructional program designed to reach individual interests and levels. Pupil-composed materials are one means of personalizing reading instruction. Robert Frost is reported to have said that the materials which help a good mind achieve the freedom essential for creativity are always different for each person.[4] The language experience approach uses different personal materials for each student.

The language experience approach is a communicative *way of learning and teaching.* In the language experience approach, reading occurs in a communication context and words are introduced, not in isolation, but in conjunction with a thought to be expressed. The child realizes that the printed words and sentences are a representation of an event or thought he already understands or has experienced. Dechant comments on the role of communication in reading:

---

[4]Sidney Cox, *A Swinger of Birches: A Portrait of Robert Frost* (New York: Collier Books, 1961), p. 53.

Communication is the heart of the language arts. Without communication listening or reading cannot occur. Reading takes place only when the child shares the ideas that the communicator intends to convey.[5]

In the language experience approach the child communicates personally through the medium of print.

Communication requires effective use of language, and it is a goal of the language experience approach to develop children's language power by providing a rich language environment and the opportunity to articulate their thoughts. Allen refers to raising a child's level of sensitivity to his environment and heightening his awareness of language as a means of expressing his knowledge of his world.[6] Directed language study starts at the present level of language development of the learner. In order to promote communication, the teacher must accept the language of the children and not block their speech through an emphasis on correction in the early stages of reading instruction.

The language experience approach is a creative *way of learning and teaching.* Creative thinking is an essential component in this approach to learning since children conceptualize thoughts and feelings through spoken and written language. Divergent responses are encouraged, accepted, and valued as children express themselves in the process of producing reading materials. Therefore, the child's role as a producer of personal materials for reading makes creative thinking a natural part of the learning act.

Teachers who seek to develop creativity realize that the classroom environment must be one which provides stimuli for and acceptance of creative thinking. The elementary school years are critical in the development of creative talent. Wilt comments on the teacher's role in freeing children to create: "First, you must believe that if a child is really to create something it must grow out of frequent opportunities to experiment and grope for his own best way to express his idea."[7] Teachers who use the language experience approach must believe that each child has some potential for creating and that he can express his creative efforts through the medium of language.

In classrooms where children's stories and language are accepted and valued, further expression is facilitated. A perfect final product is not the goal as much as is the *process of* creating and communicating through spoken and written language. The teacher has the responsibility for providing the stimuli for creativity and must realize that in order to facilitate creating through language that children must have the opportunity to hear creative language models of others and to use language creatively in their own expression of ideas.

[5]Emerald V. Dechant, *Improving the Teaching of Reading,* 2d Ed. (Englewood Cliffs, N.J.: Prentice-Hall, Inc., 1970), p. 111.

[6]R. Van Allen, *Attitudes and the Art of Teaching Reading* (Washington, D.C.: National Education Association, 1965), pp. 3–12.

[7]Miriam E. Wilt, *Creativity in the Elementary School* (New York: Appleton-Century-Crofts, 1959), p. 8.

The language experience approach is a purposeful *way of learning and teaching.* The role of purpose in learning has been well established by learning theorists and educators. In the language experience approach, learning is purposeful when pupils feel a need to communicate through language activities. Language experience reading starts with and values communication. To communicate is the reason to read and to write. The language experience learner views reading and writing as tools and processes for communication. Having important things to say, to read, and to write will be necessary for language experience learning. When a child has a personal stake in or purpose for learning to read, that purpose can have positive effects on his learning.

The language experience approach stresses the role of functional reading very early in the total reading program. Functional reading, which uses reading as a tool for learning as distinguished from learning the skills for "how to read," constitutes one of the major aspects of a comprehensive reading program. In many school programs, functional reading does not receive much emphasis until the intermediate grades. However, functional reading is incorporated into the language experience approach in the beginning stages since the production of reading materials is often an outgrowth of classroom activities in content areas such as science and social studies. Reading activities should stem from significant class activities to maintain interest and motivation at a high level.

Linguistic Foundations for the Language Experience Approach

There is a strong linguistic rationale for teaching reading with the language experience approach. The linguistic foundations for language experience reading are related to the view that reading is a language-based process, that the nature of language as a communication system has implications for the teaching of reading as a form of language communication, that readers—even beginners and remedial students—are users of language, and that the interrelationship of oral and written language affects the reading process. Since reading is communication through written language, all reading is linguistic. However, language experience reading, more than other instructional methods, offers instruction which makes it possible to capitalize on the relationship of oral and written language.

Reading is a language-based process that is dependent upon the processing of meaning through the use of printed symbols. Definitions of reading are numerous and the definitions vary according to the degree of emphasis placed on recognition of symbols and on the importance of meaning. The definition of reading intended in this book is that of Goodman's explanation of the reading process as "the reconstruction of a message from print."[8] Meaning is an essential component in this definition. Regardless of materials and methodology employed in teaching reading, a reader must be able to process the information

---

[8]Kenneth S. Goodman, ed., *The Psycholinguistic Nature of the Reading Process* (Detroit: Wayne State University Press, 1968), p. 15.

represented by the print. Language experience reading does not change the process of reading; however, language experience reading does make it possible for the process to be more natural for the beginner.

Defining language as a symbol system for communication affects the teaching of reading in the language experience approach as communication through printed language symbols. Goodman comments: "If the written language children encounter right from the beginning is whole, real, natural, and relevant, they will be able to use their existing language competence as they learn to read."[9] Reading is an interaction of the reader's language and thought with the author's language and thought. If the reader is also the author, the beginning reading task can be made easier than when the beginner is required to read unfamiliar language. To learn language, individuals must learn a code, and fortunately, when children begin to learn the written code they already possess knowledge of the oral code.

Language is systematic and patterned. The language system includes phonology, or the sound system, as well as the orthography, the written system of a language. In acquiring literacy, learners must acquire knowledge of the relationships between the phonology and the orthography of the language. In addition to the phonological system of language, there is also the system of meaning. The semantic information of a language and the syntax, or grammatical patterning, of language affect a reader's ability to read with meaning. Goodman has described the three categories of language information as:

1. *Graphophonic.* This is the information from the writing system and from the phonological system of oral language. Phonics is the name generally used when discussing the teaching of the code system of letter-sound relationships.
2. *Syntactic Information.* This is the information from grammatical structures of the language. The language user knows syntactical or sentence patterns and, therefore, is able to use this information orally before he learns to read his native language.
3. *Semantic Information.* This is information related to meaning and concepts represented by the printed words.[10]

Also basic to the linguistic foundations for the language experience approach is the concept that every reader, even the beginner, is a user of language. The language and experience children bring with them to school at ages five and six provides a foundation on which to build reading instruction. The child who comes to kindergarten and first grade not yet knowing how to read does know his native language. The remedial student who has failed at reading also knows the oral language system. The language learning of the preschool years is

---

[9]Kenneth S. Goodman, "Miscues: Windows on the Reading Process," in *Miscue Analysis,* ed. Kenneth S. Goodman (Urbana, Ill.: ERIC Clearinghouse on Reading and Communication Skills, 1973), p. 13.

[10]Kenneth S. Goodman, "Analysis of Oral Reading Miscues: Applied Psycholinguistics," *Reading Research Quarterly* 5 (Fall 1969): 17–18.

extensive, and the school beginner possesses considerable linguistic performance and competence. The existing language of the beginning reader is a foundation upon which reading instruction is built.

Language use is both receptive and productive. The preschool child learns to be both a producer and a receiver as he participates in communication situations orally as a listener and as a speaker. In the school situation he must learn two additional communication processes—one receptive and one productive—as he learns to receive printed messages in reading and to produce or encode messages in writing.

For the beginning reader, the teaching of reading should focus on helping him to make the connection between spoken and written language. The natural language of the reading material created by children in the language experience approach provides an excellent vehicle for demonstrating that language conveys meaning and for showing that the written code represents the oral code. Stauffer maintains, " . . . reading is one facet of language and one means of communication and should from the very beginning of reading instruction be taught as such through a language-experience approach."[11]

Facility in oral language is one important foundation for success in reading. Research confirms that children's achievement in oral and written language is related. Ruddell states:

> The research and opinion would suggest that an instructional program designed to develop an understanding of the relationship between the child's familiar spoken system of communication and written language would facilitate his ability to comprehend written material.[12]

Although the oral and written codes of language are closely related, they are not the same. Speech is the primary form of language; writing is a secondary symbol system and is an imperfect representation of speech. While the language experience reading material represents children's "talk written down," the process of reading is that of reconstructing a message from print. The abstractness of written language is thought to be a stumbling block to the acquisition of literacy skills. Language experience reading can lessen the abstractness of written language by using material of high comprehensibility.

In an integrated approach to teaching communication skills, the existing linguistic performance and competence in understanding and using oral language function as the starting point for developing competence in reading and writing. Teachers need to be cognizant of the interrelatedness of oral and written language and to capitalize on this interrelatedness as they teach children to communicate effectively in reading, speaking, listening, and writing.

---

[11]Russell G. Stauffer, "Certain Convictions about Reading Instruction," *Elementary English* 46 (January 1969): 86.

[12]Robert B. Ruddell, "Reading Instruction in First Grade with Varying Emphasis on the Regularity of Grapheme-Phoneme Correspondences and the Relation of Language Structure to Meaning—Extended into Second Grade," *The Reading Teacher* 20 (May 1967): 731.

Psychological Foundations of the Language Experience Approach

Since many of the psychological underpinnings of language experience learning were noted in the section on attributes, the following discussion only highlights certain psychological foundations for the language experience approach. Psychologically, the factors of success, motivation, interest, and attitude, which affect self-concept and achievement, support the use of the language experience approach. The setting for and material of language experience activities should maximize favorable conditions for learning. The language experience approach fosters success along with a favorable attitude toward reading and the self. Through successful experiences in language experience activities and through the individually created materials, a healthy self-image is promoted. The motivation to read which is generated by the stories and books produced by children is maintained through the pride of authorship and through the recognition which comes from classroom displays and sharing of those productions.

Language experience learning has a humanistic quality evident in the respect for and acceptance of the learner as he is. This respect and acceptance means respect and acceptance for the experience, the thinking, the culture, and the language that the learner brings with him to the school setting. The humanistic quality of the language experience approach is also demonstrated by the belief that the learner can participate in determining the substance of his learning.

Summary

The unique feature of the language experience approach is the use of reading materials created by the learner about his experiences and expressed in his language patterns. The teaching of reading in the language experience approach is integrated with the other communication skills in an instructional framework which stresses the personal, communicative, creative, and purposeful nature of this approach.

The linguistic base for the language experience approach rests upon a definition of reading as the processing of written language and upon a view of the reader as a user of language. The psychological base of the approach rests upon a view of the actively involved learner and on the powerful and favorable effect of successful language experience learning on interest, attitude, motivation, and self-concept.

Suggested Readings

Ashton-Warner, Sylvia. *Teacher.* New York: Simon & Schuster, Inc., 1963. A personal account of Mrs. Ashton-Warner's experiences teaching Maori children in New Zealand, this book presents an inspiring philosophy of the language experience approach.

Hall, MaryAnne. "Linguistically Speaking, Why Language Experience," *The Reading Teacher* 25 (January 1972): 328–31. Linguistic reasons for using the language experience approach for beginning readers are presented.

Lee, Dorris M., and Allen, R. V. *Learning to Read through Experience*. New York: Appleton-Century-Crofts, 1963, Chapter 1. The first chapter of Lee and Allen's book stresses the interrelatedness of the communication skills and elaborates a child's concept of reading in a language-experience framework.

Spache, George D., and Spache, Evelyn B. *Reading in the Elementary School*. New York: Allyn & Bacon, Inc., 1973, Chapter 7. The language experience approach is defined, and the advantages and limitations are discussed.

Stauffer, Russell G. *The Language Experience Approach to the Teaching of Reading*. New York: Harper and Row, Publishers, 1970. Dr. Stauffer presents a thorough discussion of both the philosophy and the implementation of language experience teaching.

chapter two

The Language Experience Approach in the Total Reading Program

The language experience approach in the total school reading program can be studied from several perspectives. In this chapter after a brief explanation of the evolvement of the approach, the approach is discussed as an approach for prereading and initial reading instruction, a supplement to other approaches beyond the beginning stages, an approach for remedial readers, an approach for culturally disadvantaged children, and as a way of instructing adult illiterates.

Also included in this chapter is a discussion of this approach in relation to the goals of an elementary reading and language arts program. The remaining chapters contain specific suggestions for instruction related to the preceding classifications.

The Evolvement of the Language Experience Approach

The beginnings of the language experience approach can be traced to the old sentence and story methods popular in the middle of the nineteenth century and to the use of experience story material in the progressive education movement of the 1930s. Hildreth has presented an excellent historical perspective on the evolution of the language experience approach from its classroom origins around 1900 through the studies investigating the approach from 1926 to 1965.[1] She notes that the term "experience method" did not appear until 1934 and that the designation "language experience" was not used until considerably later.

When Sylvia Ashton-Warner wrote about her work in New Zealand, she aroused new interest in the language experience approach in the United States.[2] Language experience reading surfaced significantly with the work of R. Van Allen in the San Diego, California schools in the 1950s.

Through the 1960s, the number of children instructed with the language experience approach increased considerably. The National First Grade Studies, the largest research project ever in beginning reading, included language experience as one of the major approaches studied.[3] From Delaware to New York, Texas to Colorado, and Pennsylvania to California language experience programs were employed.

In the decade of 1960s the language experience approach had arrived as one accepted way of teaching reading as evidenced by inclusion of discussion of this approach in textbooks on the teaching of reading, by attention given to the approach at reading conferences, and by inclusion of this method in research studies. As the amount of and interest in sociolinguistic and psycholinguistic study has grown, the theoretical rationale supporting the use of the language experience approach has become more substantial. The need for appropriate materials for the learners not of the mainstream culture has also supported the use of language experience reading. The informal open education movement in British schools has also contributed to the acceptance of the setting which is conducive to language experience learning.

Since the beginning of the 1970s, language experience teaching has received more attention in methods textbooks than ever before, and more teacher education at both the preservice and inservice levels has been devoted to this approach.

The Language Experience Approach for Beginners

The major application of the language experience approach is as a way of teaching prereading and beginning reading. The beginning reading stage is a crucial one since later attitudes and achievement are influenced by a child's progress and reactions to initial instruction. A child who experiences considerable frustration in beginning reading is very likely to develop a dislike of reading which will be a barrier to his progress at later stages. The role of success in learning to read is extremely important, and the language experience approach stresses success as the beginning reader is able to read his dictated stories since he is certain of the content of these stories.

[1]Gertrude Hildreth, "Experience Related Reading for School Beginners," *Elementary English* 42 (March 1965):280–97.

[2]Sylvia Ashton-Warner, *Teacher* (New York: Simon and Schuster, 1963).

[3]Guy L. Bond and Robert Dykstra, "The Cooperative Program in First Grade Reading Instruction," *Reading Research Quarterly* 2 (Summer 1967):5–142.

As a child first learns to read, he learns to recognize printed symbols and to associate the printed language with meanings built up through his previous experiences. A child enters school with considerable competence in oral language, and instruction in reading should be integrally related to his existing speech development. Before a child can comprehend the printed symbols of reading material, he must first be familiar with the oral language symbols and patterns which the printed words represent. The words and syntactical patterns a child encounters in beginning reading should be those which are already in his listening and speaking background. If the child has already learned the meaning of the words and is already familiar with the sentence patterns he sees in print, he can relate the printed symbols to concepts and to language already known.

In addition to stressing the relationship of reading to speaking, the language experience approach relates reading to writing and provides children with the opportunity to write extensively. The reports of the National First Grade Studies indicated that attention to writing experiences in conjunction with reading instruction is valuable. Dykstra notes that: "There is evidence that a writing component is an effective addition to a primary reading program."[4] Hildreth explains the advantages of correlating reading instruction with writing in the following statements:

> Learning to read is reinforced by simultaneous experience in writing.
>
> In writing familiar language patterns, the young writer creates material to read expanding the amount of reading material that it is easy to understand because it reflects the child's own ideas, vocabulary, and modes of expression.
>
> Writing furnishes practice in using words in meaningful sentences, strengthening the association between word forms and their meaning, and the child's familiarity with sentence patterns.[5]

Other evidence supporting early attention to writing comes from the investigations of reading prior to grade one. Durkin reported that children who learned to read early often expressed interest in learning to write before expressing interest in reading and that writing often was a factor in learning to read.[6] Hall, Moretz, and Statom found that preschool children learned to write before learning to read and that the writing done by preschool children was an effort to communicate.[7] Language experience instruction can capitalize on writing as a tool of communication.

---

[4]Robert Dykstra, "Summary of the Second-Grade Phase of the Cooperative Research Program in Primary Reading Instruction," *Reading Research Quarterly* 4 (Fall 1968): 65.

[5]Gertrude Hildreth, "Early Writing as an Aid to Reading," *Elementary English* 40 (January 1963): 15, 18.

[6]Dolores Durkin, "A Language Arts Program for Pre-First Children: Two year Achievement Report," *Reading Research Quarterly* 5 (Summer 1970): 534–565.

[7]MaryAnne Hall, Sara A. Moretz, and Jodellano Statom, "Writing Before Grade One— A Study of Early Writers," *Language Arts* 53 (May 1976): 582–585.

Many skills are involved in learning to read, and any approach to initial instruction must give attention to developing interest in reading, to building a reading vocabulary, to getting meaning from reading material, to developing skills for attacking unfamiliar words, and to teaching left-to-right progression across a line of print. In both the prereading and initial reading stages, attention also must be given to extending facility in oral language and to enriching the experience backgrounds since the ability to comprehend reading material is based on pupils' ability to understand oral language and on their experiences.

The language experience approach builds interest in reading through personal involvement and motivation in the creation of materials by the pupils. A sight vocabulary is built, not through reading basal textbooks, but by learning to recognize words used in individual and class stories. Comprehension is present since the content was meaningful when first expressed through speech. Some instruction in word attack skills is begun as pupils notice the beginnings and endings of words and as they analyze some of the words in their word banks (see chapters 5 and 8) for similar phonetic elements. Children's attention is called to left-to-right progression in reading as the teacher reads the group experience stories aloud and helps children read their individual stories.

In initial reading instruction, the pupil-composed materials include both group and individual experience stories and both group and individual word banks. A group experience story is a record of some common experience or topic of interest which is discussed by the pupils and is written by the teacher. A personal story is dictated to the teacher who records or types it for the child to use as his reading material. Individual word banks are built as a child identifies words in the group experience stories and in his own stories. Words are written on separate cards or slips of paper to be kept by each child for his word bank. These banks can tell the teacher which words are in the child's sight vocabulary and can be used as examples for instruction in phonics. Group word banks can be compiled as the class studies different classifications of words. For example, there could be categories of animal words, color words, descriptive words, action words, and others.

In beginning reading as well as at higher levels, a writing center is an important part of the classroom environment, and children's literature is a part of the total reading and language program. The writing center functions as a stimulus for independent creative writing and for following up language study as materials and ideas for creating stories are displayed. The literature experiences contribute to the motivation for reading and provide invaluable language enrichment.

Instruction in reading is started by having a child dictate a story or by writing a group experience story with the total class. However, in the early stages of instruction, it should be remembered that such instruction will have different emphases and values for different children. What is for some children a prereading experience is for other children a beginning reading activity. With the first stories some children will learn to read some words. Other children will be able to recognize likenesses and differences in printed words but will not be able to read individual words immediately. For some children the most important contribution the early stories can offer is helping them to see that their spoken ideas can be put into written form. Other children may profit most from the oral discussion which precedes the writing of the story. For all children the meaning of the written story should be clear.

When used as the major approach to beginning reading, the language experience approach can be used without systematic use of conventional instructional textbooks until pupils are reading at an advanced first grade level. At this level of reading development, the language experience approach is used as a supplement to or in combination with reading textbooks or in a program of individualized reading in trade books. The combined approach is discussed in a later section.

Research confirms that language experience reading can be one effective way of teaching beginning reading. In a review of thirteen research studies on the language experience approach from 1926 to 1965, Hildreth reported positive results for this approach in eleven instances.[8] When achievement scores in reading were compared in a study of the basal reader, individualized, and language experience approaches in San Diego County, California, the language experience approach was found to be as effective as the other two approaches in the primary grades.[9] In the National First Grade Studies, the language experience approach was found to be an effective means of teaching beginning reading.[10] One reason for the effectiveness of the language experience approach was noted by Hahn who commented that the time provided for purposeful writing, speaking, and listening in conjunction with wide reading contributed to the reading achievement of pupils using the language experience approach.[11] In looking at all of the research studies, one should remember that the actual instructional procedures varied from classroom to classroom and from study to study.

The Language Experience Approach in Combination with Other Approaches

In the total elementary reading program, the language experience approach has many advantages when employed in combination with other approaches. While teachers may not want to rely on the language experience approach as the major means of reading instruction beyond the beginning stages, they will want to incorporate many of its aspects. The high degree of personal involvement and the functional application of reading, speaking, listening, and writing are features which strongly support the use of language experience beyond the initial reading stage. In fact, the activities suggested in chapters 3–9 can be

---

[8]Hildreth, "Experience Related Reading."

[9]R. Van Allen, "More Ways Than One," *Childhood Education* 38 (November 1961): 108–111.

[10]Bond and Dykstra, "The Cooperative Research Program."

[11]Harry T. Hahn, "Three Approaches to Beginning Reading Instruction—ITA, Language Experience and Basic Readers—Extended to Second Grade," *The Reading Teacher* 20 (May 1967): 715.

easily incorporated into the language experience framework as a corollary to other approaches.

A number of authorities have commented on the value of an enriched reading program which combines features of various approaches. One of the major findings of the National First Grade Studies was that any approach which is enriched with features of other approaches produces better reading achievement than the use of one approach exclusively.[12] Stauffer and Hammond reported that the language experience approach which was effective in grade one continued to be effective at the second grade level.[13] They found that the pupils taught with the language experience approach developed greater facility in written communication than did those taught with the basal reader approach. Kendrick and Bennett also found the language experience approach to be effective through the second grade.[14] Vilscek, Cleland, and Bilka noted that pupils taught with the language experience approach through the second grade could demonstrate superiority in comprehension of concepts and in reading in the content areas of science, social studies, and arithmetic. They felt that the diversity of reading diets probably contributed to this superiority.[15]

As children move beyond the initial stages of instruction, personally created reading materials have serious limitations for providing a complete reading program. Exposure to other types of reading materials must be provided. Many of the enrichment suggestions in manuals of basal readers can be combined with the ideas of the following chapters. The basal reading program can provide a systematic development of reading skills, while the language experience activities can add personal involvement and application of language skills.

Individualized reading which features the wide reading of library materials, pupil-teacher conferences, and self-selection can be combined with language experience activities. Some teachers who use the language experience approach in beginning reading move into an individualized program when children have acquired a sufficiently large reading vocabulary to read simple library books. The pupil-teacher conference is featured in the language experience method with the individual experience stories and in individualized reading discussions. Flexible grouping in the individualized program allows for formation of interest groups as children talk about their independent reading and as they share their personal stories with each other. The suggestions for working with literature in chapter 6 will be helpful in combining independent individualized reading with language experience activities.

[12]Bond and Dykstra, "Cooperative Research Program."

[13]Russell G. Stauffer and W. Dorsey Hammond, "The Effectiveness of Language Arts and Basic Reader Approaches to First Grade Reading Instruction," *The Reading Teacher* 20 (May 1967): 740–46.

[14]William M. Kendrick and Clayton L. Bennett, "A Comparative Study of Two First Grade Language Arts Programs—Extended into Second Grade." *The Reading Teacher* 20 (May 1967): 747–55.

[15]Elaine C. Vilscek, Donald L. Cleland, and Loisanne Bilka, "Coordinating and Integrating Language Arts Instruction," *The Reading Teacher* 21 (October 1967): 10.

Some teachers who do not feel comfortable in using language experience instruction with an entire class do believe in using the language experience approach with certain students who experience difficulty with or who reject the methods or materials being used with most children. One type of combined program then is to use the language experience approach for some students while using different methods with other students. Teachers who are reluctant to teach reading with the language experience approach may use some of the language experience activities as part of the language arts curriculum.

Another possibility for combining language experience reading with the total curriculum is to use the creation of reading materials as a part of content area instruction. The purpose of listening, speaking, reading, and writing as tools for communication can be well demonstrated by the functional use of these processes through projects which stress personal involvement and creative language use. The materials created can contribute to content area learning for all levels of students, and they can provide appropriate reading materials for poor readers since the content area texts are usually too advanced for the poor readers. Much content can be presented orally with children's interpretations recorded, and then the language experience procedures can be followed for reading instruction.

When the language experience approach is combined with other approaches, emphasis is placed on developing facility in written language, on enriching the speaking and writing vocabularies as well as the reading vocabulary, and on providing integration of reading skills with other facets of communication at the higher levels. The personal, communicative, creative, and purposeful attributes of the language experience approach also operate when this approach is used in combination with other approaches and materials. In a combined program beyond the primary grades the pupil-composed materials are not used as much for reading as for stimulating creative expression, for developing power in communicating in spoken and written language, and for providing motivation for using the skills of written expression.

The contribution of language experience learning beyond the early stages is probably more to writing than to reading. Educators have probably done a better job of teaching reading than of teaching writing in the elementary schools. Many children (not to mention countless adults) who read quite well find writing clearly and expressively a difficult task. When many experiences in writing are offered in a language experience framework along with the language experience philosophy of creativity and acceptance, the hope is that effective written communication will be evidenced by students.

The Language Experience Approach for Remedial Readers

The language experience approach has merit for remedial readers who have experienced frustration in reading with conventional or traditional approaches. The psychological rationale for the language experience approach seems particularly significant for remedial readers since these children often exhibit a negative attitude toward reading and may reject remediation attempts which use more of the same type of instruction which was unsuccessful in the past. Attitude, success, and motivation are of primary importance in working with remedial readers. For pupils who possess a negative attitude toward reading as a result of repeated frustration and failure, the use of personally created materials can remove the fear of failure. The language experience approach can promote a favorable attitude toward reading and can develop a high degree of personal involvement with intrinsic motivation as students experience success through the reading of their experience stories.

Johnson states five fundamental principles of learning which underlie working with remedial readers:

1. Learning begins with the known.
2. Learning proceeds from concrete to abstract.
3. Learning demands active participation.
4. Learning should be goal directed.
5. Learning is an individual matter.[16]

The language experience approach does begin with known material which is easily decoded and understood, does provide concrete materials as the starting point, does actively involve the learner, does help the student set attainable goals, and does approach reading in an individual manner with concern for a personal involvement in the reading situation.

The linguistic rationale for the language experience approach also applies to remedial reading students. The view of reading as processing of ideas presented in written language should underlie remedial instruction. Often the remedial student has been given narrow and distorted reading instruction which has focused on small units of language and on isolated skills without a meaningful language base. Meaningful language contained in sentence and story units can help remedial students to use semantic and syntactical clues in reading as well as the clues contained in the graphophonic information.

The descriptions of the language experience approach and the techniques described in chapters 3–8 can be adapted for remedial reading instruction. The basic idea of starting with the pupil's language to create reading materials is again followed when this approach is used with remedial readers. Using the spoken language of the reader is an advantage since the remedial student has usually advanced in oral language beyond the language of the textbooks on his instructional level. For example, the fifth grade child who is reading on a first grade reading level will be more advanced in his oral language than the language employed in a first grade reader, and he will have little interest in the content of a book designed for a child of six.

When using language experience reading with remedial readers it is impor-

---

[16]Marjorie S. Johnson, "Basic Considerations in Corrective Instruction," in *Corrective Reading in the Classroom: Perspectives in Reading No. 7*, ed. Marjorie S. Johnson and Roy A. Kress (Newark, Del.: International Reading Association, 1966), pp. 64–68.

tant to remember that although the procedures will be similar to those recommended for younger students, the content will be quite different. The principle
of using the concerns of the students remains, but those concerns will differ
considerably at different age levels. Among the motivating ideas which often
appeal to older students are the topics of cars, motorcycles, sports, music, and
entertainers. One teacher has reported successful results when using the adver-
tising material from automobile agencies. Another has reported that the use of
the explanatory material on favorite record albums of students was successful
in motivating students to produce language experience materials. Sports pictures from magazines and newspapers can also lead to the creation of individual
and group stories. Books students create about favorite sports or entertainment
figures are usually popular reading materials.

Language experience for remedial students often serves as a bridge to other
reading materials. After the student has experienced some success through
personal experience stories, he can move on to other materials, or the language
experience procedures can be integrated with a combined approach. As he
works with experience stories, needed work in skills can be provided by studying words used in his stories which illustrate the particular patterns to be
mastered. Comprehension also can be developed through the personal experience stories, especially for those students who "word-call" instead of reading
with meaning.

The author acknowledges the need for careful evaluation of each remedial
reader's strengths and weaknesses and realizes that the instructional approach
selected must be adapted to the particular reading needs of each student.
Specific deficiencies must be diagnosed and appropriate instruction offered.
The language experience approach is not suggested as a panacea for all remedial cases, but it is recommended as one approach which may help some children with reading difficulties, especially from the standpoint of developing
favorable attitudes and for illustrating the relationship between oral and written language.

The Language Experience Approach for the Culturally Disadvantaged

The language experience approach seems particularly appropriate for use
with disadvantaged children since language experience teaching makes it possible to have materials which match both the experiences and language patterns
of disadvantaged children.

Typically, culturally disadvantaged children experience considerable difficulty and frustration with traditional methods of reading instruction. As a result
of reading problems, these children are handicapped in all school activities
which require reading. The language experience approach for disadvantaged
children is of greatest relevance in the beginning stages of instruction; however, it continues to be important for teaching communication skills at higher
levels.

A number of factors can be cited for the difficulties disadvantaged children experience in reading. Among those factors are lack of readiness for school, limited and/or different experience backgrounds, meager opportunities for oral communication in the preschool years, poor self-concept, negative attitude toward school, and a curriculum which is foreign to their backgrounds and interests. Of particular importance in reading is the language background of the learner. While the language spoken by some disadvantaged learners is a non-standard variety of English, there is sufficient language learning for initiating reading instruction. For the divergent dialect speaker, language experience materials can provide materials using the language patterns of the learner. Serwer advocates the use of "language engendered by the experience and verbalization of the child as a basis for the reading process." She elaborates further,

> It is safe to say for *beginning* literacy that the child must learn to read in his own dialect or in his first language if it is different. The most economical and rational way to accomplish this goal as well as to capture his interest and to engage him on an appropriate level of concept development is by using his own verbalization, ensconced in his ideation, his idiom, his rhythm, and his style. If the child's language is used and instruction in decoding is based on this language, it is reasonable to assume that early reading would be less prone to failure.[17]

One significant advantage of the language experience approach is the use of materials which are written in the language of the learner. A child who speaks a nonstandard variety of the language may experience difficulty with conventional materials written in standard English. However, when language experience materials are used, there can be a match between the reading materials and the spoken language of the reader.

Of crucial importance is the acceptance of the disadvantaged child's existing language as reading materials are developed. The intent is to use the present level of language development as the medium of communication through which he learns to read. For example, the following story was dictated by a child in a city slum:

> Her is Mom.
> Her braids my hair.
> Her cleans around.
> Her shouts me to watch Eddie.
> Nothing else.[18]

For this child to have her story recorded using "she" for "her" in the first two sentences would probably result in her reading the printed word "she" as "her," thus resulting in confusion of word forms. If the pronoun "she" is not in her oral language background, it should not *at this stage* be used in the reading

---

[17]Blanche L. Serwer, "Linguistic Support for a Method of Teaching Beginning Reading to Black Children," *Reading Research Quarterly* 4 (Summer 1969): 458.

[18]"Poignant Drawings are Helping Slum Children Learn to Read," *The Washington Post*, August 28, 1966, Sec. F., p. 13. © *The Washington Post*.

material. A caution should be noted here. The materials used should be written with standard spelling even though the child's vocabulary and syntax will be recorded. For example, if a child says "nes" for "nest," "nest" should be written, but the child can still pronounce it "nes."

Goodman hypothesizes that the biggest problem dialect speakers face in reading instruction is not the use of a divergent dialect but is the rejection of their speech by teachers. He maintains:

> The only special disadvantage which speakers of low-status dialects suffer in learning to read is one imposed by teachers and schools. Rejection of their dialects and educators' confusion of linguistic difference with linguistic deficiency interferes with the natural process by which learning to read is acquired and undermines the linguistic self-confidence of divergent speakers.[19]

The divergent dialect speaker must be recognized as a user of language, and the language he uses must be accepted and built upon in teaching him the skills of literacy. It is possible to use the language children already possess as a bridge between oral communication and written language. Recognition of reading as language processing should focus attention on the tasks confronting a reader who must process language information encoded in a language system which he finds difficult to relate to his known oral language system. It should be noted that there is a mismatch factor between spoken and written language for all children since written language is never an exact representation of the oral code, but the difference between the two is greater for linguistically different children.

The need for realistic reading programs which offer maximum opportunity to develop the culturally disadvantaged child's ability to communicate is pressing. The language experience approach is one means of providing meaningful reading content. A moving compilation of writings of ghetto children is found in *The Me Nobody Knows* edited by Stephen M. Joseph.[20] In *Hooked on Books* by Daniel Fader,[21] personal writing was one feature of a program developed to reach disadvantaged and delinquent youth through exposure to paperback books. The examples included in these two sources show dramatically the relevancy and impact of personal writing for the disadvantaged.

Stauffer and Cramer report,

> When, . . . , the disadvantaged person is given an opportunity to read accounts that he has produced, which reflect his thinking about things important to him, and which are a part of his direct experience, his progress is often dramatic.[22]

---

[19]Kenneth S. Goodman with Catherine S. Buck, "Dialect Barriers to Reading Comprehension Revisited," *The Reading Teacher* 27 (October 1973): 6–7.

[20]Stephen M. Joseph, ed., *The Me Nobody Knows* (New York: Avon Books, 1969).

[21]Daniel N. Fader, *Hooked on Books: Program and Proof* (New York: Berkley Publishing Corporation, 1968).

[22]Russell G. Stauffer and Ronald L. Cramer, "Reading Specialists in an Occupational Training Program," *The Reading Teacher* 20 (March 1967): 528.

The language experience approach can be an intensive effort to compensate for and to alleviate the major problems of a lack of readiness for reading, the inappropriate story content of reading textbooks, and the oral language differences which handicap culturally disadvantaged children in reading. Through stimulating experiences and intense personal involvement, the language experience approach can introduce reading to disadvantaged children in a personal, communicative, creative, and purposeful manner.

The Language Experience Approach for Adult Illiterates

In recent years attention to the problems of adults who are functionally illiterate has increased. Statistics confirm that a large number of adults in the United States are classified as functionally illiterate. The definition of functional illiteracy may vary from inability to read above a certain grade level (often cited are fourth or fifth or eighth grade levels) or a lack of schooling beyond four or five years to a negative response to the question, "Can you read or write?" Depending on definition, the number of illiterates seems to vary from ten to thirty million—yet, in addition to these figures, there are probably many unidentified illiterates. Regardless of definition, it is certain that many adults are in great need of programs designed to develop reading ability.

As the popularity of the language experience approach has increased, applications of this approach have been made to adult populations. The advantages of language experience reading for an adult illiterate are those stated earlier for elementary students. The language facility that adults have is an asset drawn upon in teaching reading, and the desire adults have for relevant content can be met through language experience learning related to occupational concerns and aspirations as well as to other survival needs. It is possible with language experience learning to have appropriate, meaningful, and functional material.

Adaptations of language experience approach based on interests of adult students can be made with use of driver's manuals, banking and credit forms, labels, cooking instructions, TV guides, road signs, application forms, menus, bus schedules, and the like. All of these materials would fit into the "survival" category which would be of high priority in a basic literacy program. The materials mentioned could be used for oral discussion which then would lead to the writing of students' ideas. The recorded ideas would then be used to teach reading.

An educator noted for his work with illiterates in Latin America, Paulo Friere, stresses that the foundation for humanistic literacy learning is authentic dialogue among the people. The dialogue then becomes the base from which literacy is learned. The examples he gives of books composed by illiterate peasants whom he calls "sowers of words" are in his words, "simple, poetic, free" and "profound and elegant."[23]

---

[23]Paulo Friere, *Cultural Action for Freedom* (Cambridge, Mass: Center for Study of Development and Social Change and *Harvard Educational Review*, 1970), pp. 24–25.

He contrasts the authentic creations of the people with the dull materials often used with illiterates:

> Intellectualist prejudices and above all class prejudices are responsible for the naive and unfounded notions that the people cannot write their own texts, or that a tape of their conversations is valueless since their conversations are impoverished of meaning. Comparing what the "sowers of words" said in the above references with what is generally written by specialist authors of reading lessons, we are convinced that only someone with very pronounced lack of taste or a lamentable scientific incompetency would choose the specialists' texts.[24]

Friere strongly advocates drawing the material for instruction from the concerns of those to be instructed. While the structure of the teaching he advocates is not identical to language experience procedures described in this book, much of the basic philosophy is similar.

A major point to remember in instructing adults is that the instruction should be perceived by the adult learners as functional and pragmatic. Content of language experience programs then will not be predetermined but will be developed according to the concerns of the individuals in a particular group. Skill instruction and acquisition of a reading vocabulary along with reading for meaning must be included in adult reading instruction, but this instruction can be initiated with language experience situations.

The Goals of the Language Experience Approach

The goals of the language experience approach are related to the goals of both reading and language arts instruction. The broad primary goal of language experience instruction is to develop students' abilities to communicate through reading and through language. As an approach to reading instruction, the language experience must, like any approach to reading instruction, build children's reading vocabularies, establish effective strategies for word attack, develop comprehension ability, and promote a favorable attitude toward and a permanent interest in reading.

In a statement of goals for the language arts, James Smith stresses the need for relevant daily experiences for children to meet the goals. While it is not the intent of this book to examine in detail the content of a language arts program, the importance of language experience activities in the total language arts programs should be recognized. Smith identifies the goals of language arts programs as:

1. Each child needs to experience language (remarkably) in dynamic and relevant ways, all day, every day, so he can communicate comfortably in every way open to him, and without unnecessary pressures.

---

[24]Ibid.

2. Each child must acquire necessary communication skills so that he may express himself effectively in all media.
   a. to listen effectively and for a variety of purposes
   b. to speak effectively in many kinds of social situations
   c. to spell acceptably as a social courtesy
   d. to write legibly and with ease
   e. to learn correct word usage as a social courtesy
   f. to use capitalization and punctuation as social courtesy
   g. to use grammar correctly as a social courtesy
   h. to use reference material effectively
   i. to use word forms correctly

3. Each child needs to come to appreciate the beauty of language itself, the effective use of words, and creative ways they may help him express his own original thoughts.

4. Each child needs to find such satisfaction in his communication experiences that he will develop a healthy attitude toward communicating in all media and will develop his communication skills even without the assistance of the teacher.[25]

Applegate offers the following statement of the goals of the language arts:

To use words responsibly
To think clearly
To listen imaginatively
To speak effectively
To read thoughtfully
To write creatively
To use mechanics powerfully
To regard good English respectively
To acquaint children with the best (literature).[26]

The preceding goal statements reflect the integration of reading and language instruction. The language experience approach requires that experiences form the base for the use and development of communication abilities in both oral and written language. A successful language experience reading program teaches both reading and language arts skills in situations in which communication is necessary and in which communication abilities are continually being expanded.

Summary

The language experience approach has been increasingly accepted in recent years as a valid method for teaching reading and communication skills. The

[25]James A. Smith, *Adventures in Communication* (Boston: Allyn and Bacon, 1972), pp. 91–93.
[26]Mauree Applegate, *Easy in English* (Evanston, Ill.: Row, Peterson and Company, 1960), p. 8.

language experience approach is employed for prereading and initial reading instruction, for remedial readers, for culturally disadvantaged children, as a supplement to other approaches, and occasionally with adult illiterates. The teacher must accept the students' existing level of language development and their language patterns as they create their personal reading materials. The primary goal of reading and language arts instruction in the language experience framework is to develop the ability to communicate in all facets of language.

Suggested Readings

Allen, R. Van. *Attitudes and the Art of Teaching Reading.* Washington, D.C.: National Education Association, 1965. This pamphlet includes background information for the teacher as well as classroom profiles of kindergarten, primary, and remedial reading classes.

Hall, MaryAnne. *The Language Experience Approach for the Culturally Disadvantaged.* Newark, Del.: The International Reading Association, 1972. This pamphlet is a review of research on the language experience approach as it relates to the culturally disadvantaged. In addition to an analysis of the research in the areas of readiness, word attack, vocabulary, comprehension, spelling, and creative writing, research needs are discussed.

Hildreth, Gertrude. "Experience Related Reading for School Beginners," *Elementary English* 42 (March 1965): 280–97. Hildreth offers a thorough presentation of the historical background of the language experience approach as well as giving citations of the early research and programs related to this approach.

Kohl, Herbert A. *Teaching the "Unteachable."* New York: The New York Review, 1967. Kohl includes many examples of the writings of disadvantaged children to illustrate that children can write creatively and expressively when provided the freedom and encouragement to do so without the drudgery and dislike frequently associated with English composition.

Serwer, Blanche L. "Linguistic Support for a Method of Teaching Beginning Reading to Black Children," *Reading Research Quarterly* 7 (Summer 1969): 449–67. Serwer explores the linguistic rationale for the language experience approach for the initial teaching of reading to disadvantaged children.

Stauffer, Russell G. *The Language Experience Approach to the Teaching of Reading.* New York: Harper and Row, Publishers, 1970. Procedures for the language experience approach are described in detail. In addition to much attention to beginning reading, applications to higher levels are discussed.

Wilson, Robert M. *Diagnostic and Remedial Reading for Classroom and Clinic,* 2d Ed. Columbus, Ohio: Charles E. Merrill Publishing Company, 1972. The topics of diagnosis and remediation are the major emphasis of this informative source on working with problem readers. Numerous language experience applications for remediation are featured.

chapter three

Experience Stories

One of the major types of reading material in the language experience approach is the experience story. Both individual and group language experience stories are widely used. A variation of the group experience story is the group book which is composed from separate pages by different children about a selected topic. In this chapter individual experience stories, group experience stories, and group books are discussed with emphasis upon the procedures for developing and using them in the teaching of reading and language skills.

The _process_ of developing and using the story is the most important consideration, not the final product or the form of the story itself. The familiarization with the procedures should free the teacher to concentrate on the _communication_ process in the _formulation_ of the content, in the _recording_ of the story, and in the _reading experiences_ connected with the story. Tiedt and Tiedt define writing as "thought transferred to paper."[1] Encouraging thinking is essential in the process of creating experience stories if children are to view the writing process as the use of letter symbols to record thoughts. Ideas, not mechanics of writing, should be the major concern.

In this chapter many of the comments for using experience stories apply to the beginning stages of reading instruction, but

---

[1] Iris M. Tiedt and Sidney W. Tiedt, _Contemporary English in the Elementary School_ (Englewood Cliffs, N.J.: Prentice-Hall, Inc., 1967), p. 145.

adaptations can be made for higher levels. The development of experience stories at any level follows the sequence of having children express thoughts through speaking, the recording of these thoughts in printed language, and finally the reading of the story, with emphasis on communication in each step.

As children mature in language skills and as the number of words they are able to write independently increases, the experience story becomes less teacher-directed and more pupil-directed. The focus changes from complete dependence upon the teacher as recorder to limited teacher assistance and finally to independent creative writing. Even though the level of material and difficulty of content increases, the values of personal authorship remain. At higher levels, the written story is used less for teaching reading skills and vocabulary and is used more for furthering creative expression through written language. In chapter 4 creative writing in the language experience approach is described in detail.

Group Experience Stories

In the development of a group experience story the children participate in an event or discussion of an event or a selected topic. The children's ideas are recorded and then used for reading material. The teacher must give consideration to motivation, oral discussion of the experience, recording, reading, and follow-up activities. (Follow-up activities related to prereading skills are discussed in chapter 7, while other specific skills are discussed in chapter 8.)

Motivation for Experience Stories

The teacher has the responsibility for providing motivating experiences which are appropriate and worthwhile. Unless story content is perceived as interesting and personal to children, experience stories can be subject to all the criticism of dull content often leveled at basal readers. Hopefully, teachers using the language experience approach will be skilled in drawing from children much lively comment which will result in highly motivating material, which is relevant for those working with it. The suggestions given here are only suggestions since it is impossible to determine the content of language experience material apart from the group and individuals involved.

Often a live animal is an excellent stimulus for language experience stories —particularly in the beginning stages. Oral discussion seems to flow naturally with animals as the stimuli.

With five-, six-, and seven-year-old children topics which center around themselves seem to be the most successful in triggering free responses. For that reason using the open-ended sentence story starters which contain "I" are recommended. For example, topics such as "I like to . . . , I wish . . . , At home I . . . , After school I . . ." are ones to which it is easy for children to respond.

Many opportunities for composing charts will occur in every classroom. Lists of classroom duties, charts of standards, letters to other classes, letters relating to field trips, and weather records are only a few examples of excellent opportunities for using experience stories related to functional situations. However, the majority of the group experience stories will be of the narrative type, which children compose creatively. Trips, pets, classroom events, pictures, holidays, and television provide springboards for discussion for chart stories.

Commercial materials can be used to motivate language experience stories. The language experience programs of the Encyclopaedia Britannica Press contain numerous ideas to help a teacher plan language experience activities.[2] The *Peabody Language Development Kits*[3] are also particularly useful in providing both pictures and ideas for experience stories. Films also serve as a source of motivation.

One technique for motivating experience stories is that of reading a children's literature story to children and then having them discuss and recall some of the ideas of that story to create an experience story. A variation of this would be to have children create their own story about the same topic but with their ideas. The children's books now available which consist of pictures but no words work well to stimulate stories composed by children.

Many teachers are successful in using pictures to get children to express ideas. If that succeeds, fine. One caution with the use of pictures is that children may tend to only describe and may not feel any personal connection with that stimulus and thus may feel less involved than when the story is more related to them.

ORAL DISCUSSION WITH EXPERIENCE STORIES

The group discussion which precedes the writing of the children's ideas provides an important language activity. The discussion experience gives children the opportunity to express and hear ideas in oral language. In discussion situations listening habits can be established, and the teacher can observe and evaluate the language facility of the children. It must be remembered, too, that extending both the experience and language backgrounds of children is a prime concern in language arts instruction.

During the discussion a number of pupils can contribute ideas, and the story produced represents the thinking of the different group members. Even when the number of pupils involved is large, the teacher can provide opportunities for all pupils to participate in this type of activity since the class will be writing many chart stories.

For some children the oral part of the language experience activities is particularly important since some children are very much in need of opportunities to increase their ability to express and understand ideas through oral language.

---

[2]Roach Van Allen, *Language Experiences in Reading* (Chicago: Encyclopaedia Britannica Press, 1974).

[3]Lloyd M. Dunn and James O. Smith, *Peabody Language Development Kits*, Levels I, II, III (Minneapolis: American Guidance Service, 1965, 1966, 1967).

The discussion often seems smoother if it is done before there is any attempt to record the comments. After the objectives of the discussion are accomplished, it seems easier to develop the written story if each child is asked to tell something he remembers or likes about the topic. After each response each child's language is then recorded. This procedure can prevent the first discussion from being disconnected because of the recording.

RECORDING OF GROUP EXPERIENCE STORIES

The teacher records the pupils' ideas on the chalkboard or on chart paper *using the language of the pupils*. These stories should reflect the oral language patterns of the group composing them, not the teacher's polishing of their language to meet her standards of "good" English. If desired, a title is selected by the children and then used in the written record. Appropriate punctuation and capitalization are used as needed. Manuscript writing is used with large letters for easy visibility with careful spacing between words so that the beginning reader can see the relationship of one written word for each spoken word. No attempt is made to control the vocabulary or to limit sentence length.

For beginners and remedial students, watching the recording is recommended in order to develop the realization that the print represents their thoughts. The recording of the story should be done immediately following the discussion so that students have reading material produced immediately. While

Ken's Pizza
We went in Miss Nancy's car.
We went inside and saw
them make dough.
We got a piece of dough.
Then we got to see how
they made the pizza.
After we saw how they
make pizza, we saw them
put it in the oven.
Then we sat down.
We ate two pieces.
We had cheese without
no macaroni.

a tape recorder may be helpful as a means for encouraging creation of stories and for motivating reading practice, taping does not provide for the observation of the process of writing to demonstrate that thoughts can be represented by printed language.

If the original recording was done on the chalkboard, which many teachers feel is faster and best for the initial lesson with an experience story, the teacher should later copy the story on primary chart paper with a felt-tip pen or marker.

READING OF EXPERIENCE STORIES

The first reading of a group experience story is usually done by the teacher immediately after the recording. For children in the initial stages of reading instruction, the teacher will emphasize the left-to-right progression across a line of print while reading the story to the group. Then, the teacher may ask the group to read the story with her. Then, a few children may volunteer to read the story individually. Probably, the motivation, oral discussion, and first reading of the story will occur in the first day's work with an experience story. Additional reading of the chart will be done on following days with some of the activities suggested below.

For prereaders and beginning readers, the second day's reading of the story is again done first by the teacher as the children watch. Next the group reads the story with the teacher and then some children read the story individually with as much teacher assistance as needed. The reading should be successful and not frustrating. Unnecessary frustration can occur when beginners are asked to read a story without first hearing it read by the teacher. I'm reminded of the student teacher who came to me saying that I had said children could read what they had written when she had taken a reading methods course with me. I went to watch her teach a "slow" group of first graders only to notice that after the excellent motivation and discussion individual children were directed to read the story and balked at this request. By simply changing the procedure to have the story read by the teacher first and then again with the children, it was possible to build successful experiences while also providing some needed repetition.

FOLLOW-UP ACTIVITIES WITH EXPERIENCE STORIES

A completed experience record is displayed in the classroom and is used again for various reading activities. In most cases, three or four days will be the maximum spent with any one chart. It is preferable to write and read many charts rather than to overdrill on a few. The group experience stories may be collected on a chart rack for reference in the following weeks. Occasionally, there may be rereading of some charts just for fun. If the charts are available in the class, many children may choose to reread the charts as a free time activity.

Duplicated copies of the group stories have many uses. Copies of the stories can be compiled into a class book which will be available in the class library or on the reading table. Word, phrase, and sentence cards which correspond with the chart can be made and children can match the cards to the story. An envelope of the words for each story in the folder in the reading corner can be made and can be used for independent practice in visual discrimination. Children can also work independently with matching words and phrases if they are given two duplicated copies and are asked to cut out individual words to match to words in the intact copy. For children who have not yet begun to read, group charts can be used to provide practice in letter recognition. Children can match letter cards to letters on charts and can name letters in the experience stories. In the follow-up activities, children can frame certain words with an index card with a window cut in it as a teacher may show words on the group chart or as she just says certain words.

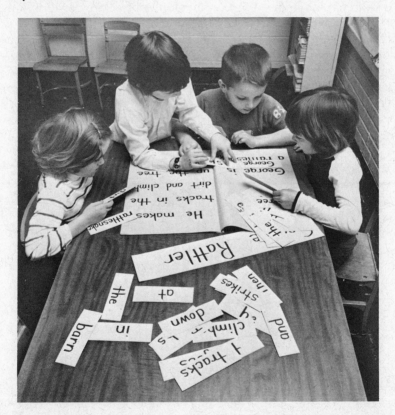

Each child should keep a folder with a copy of each group experience story and the folder will be in effect one of his reading books. On the second day of working with a group experience story, each child should be given a duplicated copy of the story. With this copy a child can underline every word he knows, match word cards to the copy, reread the story, illustrate the story, and participate in other teacher-directed activities. Additional reading practice is present when children work in pairs to read the stories to each other or when by choice they reread the stories in the folder. Dramatizing and illustrating are highly motivating creative activities for children. These can be excellent follow-up activities and can also be the motivators for creating experience stories.

In addition to the copies used at school, copies of experience stories may be taken home by children to read with their parents. A note of caution is in order here. Parents should be instructed in how to help their children with the stories and also should know how much is expected of the children. Many teachers find it advisable to send a letter to parents informing them of the procedures to be followed and of the purpose of the stories in the reading program. For beginners, teachers usually recommend that children listen to the parents read the story first before children read it with the parents and then alone. Parents usually appreciate being informed too that any underlined words are words which the child is expected to know.

The stories can also be used in the development of class or individual word banks as pupils identify words of various categories. (See pp. 62–63.) For example, a chart about the leaves in the fall could be used to start a classification of color words. "Animal" words, "action" words, "naming" words, and other categories also would evolve from the experience stories. If a child can read a word or words in a group story, those words can be added to his individual word bank.

Stauffer suggests dividing a first grade class into groups and developing experience stories with each. The pace of the instruction and the extent of follow-up activities will vary depending upon the ability of the group.[4]

AN EXAMPLE OF A GROUP EXPERIENCE STORY

The following story was dictated by a first grade class during the first week of school.

The Rabbit's Nature

> He eats carrots and cabbage.
> He's lonesome when his mother is away.
> He doesn't go anywhere.
> He looks black.

The title was a surprise to the teacher but when the child who suggested it was asked why he wanted that title, he replied, "Well, the story tells what the rabbit is like!" The story was recorded with the children's language exactly as they said it. The contractions were used since they were a part of the children's speech. No attempt was made to repeat or change vocabulary.

Often in the beginning stages, children's names are used in the writing of the story. For example, the story could have been written in a form such as: Brian said, "He eats carrots and cabbage."

---

[4]Russell G. Stauffer, *The Language-Experience Approach to the Teaching of Reading* (New York: Harper and Row, Publishers, 1970), pp. 25–36.

The motivation in this instance was the live animal. The motivation triggered a lively oral discussion which was followed by the teacher's recording of the children's dictated ideas. Next, the teacher read the story to the group, and then the children read the story with her. Additional reading of the chart occurred in the subsequent three days in conjunction with follow-up activities. Copies were made for each child and were used for follow-up activities.

OTHER APPLICATIONS OF GROUP EXPERIENCE STORIES

Although group charts may not be as widely used after the first half of grade one, some children are still operating at the prereading and initial stages of reading well into grade one and beyond. For these students, the group experience stories are particularly valuable. Most children, however, will have progressed to a combined approach using language experience materials along with basal readers and library books. Beyond the beginning stages of reading, the group chart serves as a functional language activity and can be a record of important events within the class.

Edwards describes the following five-step procedure for using the language experience approach in a group situation with remedial students who were either disadvantaged adolescents or functionally illiterate adults.

1. The teacher stimulates and guides a discussion of a topic or experience.
2. The group's ideas are recorded (by one or all members).
3. Logical sentences and paragraphs are constructed from the randomly recorded thoughts.
4. There is silent reading of the entire selection after it has been duplicated for all students.
5. A variety of follow-up activities can be conducted by small groups or individual students.[5]

The teaching of vocabulary, pronunciation, comprehension, and word attack skills is incorporated as needed in the above sequence especially at steps three and five.

The group experience story approach can be adapted for teaching manuscript writing in grade one. The teacher will need to explain that what they write will be much shorter than a chart story but that they can write their own ideas. There will be oral discussion of an experience or idea to determine the statement the children want to record. For instance, the rabbit story on p. 32 could serve as the stimulus with a short sentence such as "The rabbit hops" or "The rabbit is black" selected for the writing activity. The teacher will demonstrate on a chalkboard, large writing paper, or a transparency for the overhead projector the formation of each letter as the children reproduce the letters for

[5]Thomas J. Edwards, "The Language Experience Approach on Cultural Deprivation," *The Reading Teacher* 18 (April 1965):546–51.

their individual papers. After the writing, the sentence is read so that children feel that their writing communicates an idea. In the stages of first learning to write, the sentence will probably consist of only three or four words. As skill in writing develops, the length of sentences and the stories will increase.

Individual Experience Stories

The concept that his speech can be put into written form is a key one for a child using the language experience approach and is best developed through the personal experience story. Personal stories have the same advantages of the group stories and, in addition, probably stimulate more interest in reading because of the greater personal involvement.

Often children are familiar with the procedures for developing a group story before they compose individual stories. Therefore, they are familiar with the practice of talking about an experience or idea and seeing the thoughts encoded into written symbols which they can then read. As was true for group stories, in using individual stories the teacher must consider motivation, oral discussion, recording and reading of the stories, and follow-up activities.

Many times the motivation for individual stories is conducted with the total class or with a subgroup as the teacher presents an idea, topic, or picture as the stimulus for discussion. Oral language discussions preceding the development of individual stories are necessary to promote the language development of some pupils and to encourage thinking. Through questioning, the teacher seeks to elicit pupil interest and response. The teacher may use a picture or object to ask: "What do you see?" "What does this make you think of?" "What happened first?" "What happened next?" "What would you like to do?" Trips, pictures, individual experiences, events, literature, art work, birthdays, pets, and special interests can provide the stimuli for an individual story.

As was true with the group experience stories, the student should observe the recording of the story. A child should be encouraged to tell a story idea by idea instead of word by word. Sometimes children tend to dictate word by word thinking it may be easier for the recorder, but this pattern may result in unnatural reading.

These stories are usually recorded in manuscript writing or with a primary typewriter. Teachers may choose the form easier for themselves while recognizing that the young reader may prefer the typewritten form since it is more like the print in books. The recorded story should be in such a form as to create pride in its author. A uniform size is desirable if pupil folders of class books are to be compiled with the various stories. In some schools teacher aides or upper grade children are available to record children's dictated stories.

Immediately after the recording of an individual story, the teacher reads the story to the child. (After the beginning stages of instruction, reading by the teacher can be omitted.) The teacher and child read the story together, and then the pupil can read it alone with teacher help where needed. The next step is for the teacher to ask the child to identify the words he can read in the story.

As the child says he knows a particular word, it is written on a card for his word bank.

After children have a basic sight vocabulary, the teacher does not have to hear all the reading of all stories written by the pupils. As the language experience approach is used in connection with other approaches beyond the beginning stages, the children will read many materials in addition to the personal stories. At this time the personal stories become more important as an outlet for creative expression rather than as a means of teaching initial reading. The creative stories can be shared in small group settings so that children have an opportunity for oral reading and for hearing the creative work of their peers.

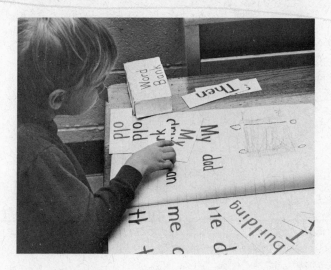

After the stories have been recorded and read with the teacher, the child is ready to work independently with his story. The types of activity which follow the reading depend upon the child's stage of development. In the beginning stages of reading, he can underline or circle those words which he can identify or which he had identified with the teacher during the first reading session. The words he can read will become part of his word bank. He can take the word cards from his bank and use them for visual discrimination practice and for practice in word recognition as he matches the words in his bank to words in his story. At later stages of development, the reader can identify the words he does *not* know. The latter procedure is followed only after he can recognize all but a few of the words in the story.

Illustrating stories is a popular activity for children and adds to the appeal of the finished product. In fact, pupil illustrations provide one of the strongest impetuses for producing personal materials. It is the illustrations, too, as well as the thoughts expressed, which contribute to the individuality of the stories. Often personal experience stories will originate from illustrations. Children's drawings can serve as the stimuli for creating a story. Teachers may find that for pupils who are reluctant to create stories that having them tell a story about their pictures is the easiest way to begin pupil authorship.

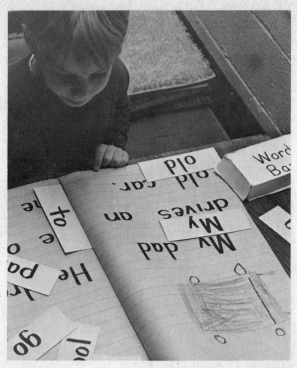

In an experimental project in the District of Columbia, Polaroid cameras were made available for teachers. The personal response to pictures of themselves triggered story production from some children who had not reacted to any other stimulus.

An idea used by some kindergarten and first grade teachers is to have an individual conference with each child the first week of school. In that conference the child is encouraged to talk about himself and the teacher writes the child's comments. At the conclusion of the conference, each child has a personal book. The book may be titled with the name of the child or titles such as "About Me," "My Story," "A Story About _____."

Often the teacher may want to display children's illustrated stories with appropriate captions on bulletin boards. A feeling of pride and achievement results when a child realizes that his story is valued enough to be used for classroom display. The bulletin board displays can stimulate children to read their stories to their classmates, thereby providing additional reading practice.

After individual stories are written, pupils can keep them in a folder. Some teachers make carbon copies when typing the stories for the children for evaluation of the child's progress or for display.

When the children have written and read the individual stories the teacher may form small groups for the purpose of sharing the stories. Oral reading expression can be stressed in this audience type situation, and personal accomplishment will be felt. The teacher is available to help with difficult words so that no child is placed in a situation where he will be unsuccessful. Listening habits are practiced in a functional situation. Children can tape their stories, and the recordings can be used in the listening center.

Individual stories can be placed in the reading corner for independent reading by the rest of the class. Occasionally, the stories can be shown with an opaque projector for reading. The teacher can invite children from another class to hear a group of children read their stories. Sometimes the stories are collected for a class book. The library shelves in the class can include a section of children's stories. In some schools, children's original stories have been placed in the school's central library collection. The motivation of the above practices is obvious.

Having blank booklets already prepared may serve as an invitation to write for some children. A few pages of blank newsprint stapled together with construction paper covers should be part of the supplies available in a writing center. Chapters 4 and 6 also contain suggestions for stimulating the writing of individual stories.

Group Books

Another popular type of pupil-developed reading material is the group book which is produced by combining the efforts of a number of pupils. Usually the group books are comprised of collections of pages on the same topic by different children. At higher levels as the group books are related to content in social studies and science, each page may deal with a different aspect of an identified topic. Some group books may be written as follow-ups to children's literature materials. Some may be collections of children's creative stories. Some will develop from class discussions, while still others will be outgrowths of study in other curriculum areas. Group books are an excellent source of pupil-composed material for the classroom reading corner.

Since group books are cooperative efforts, the motivation and preliminary discussion of the content ordinarily will be in a group setting. In the beginning stages of reading instruction, group books may consist of one sentence with an illustration for each page. For example, one first grade teacher was discussing the color red and had the children draw a picture and dictate a sentence about something which was red. The book had a red construction paper cover and was called "Red Things." Some sentences were, "The sun at night is red," "My dress is red," and "A crayon is red." At a more advanced level the books can contain more involved content about more advanced topics and are often written as committee projects related to content areas. These books can be a means of functional writing and reading when pupils use them for recording information and for reporting information to their classmates. For example, if the class had been studying a science unit on electricity, a group book on this topic could be written with each child reporting different information pertinent to the unit.

As children illustrate their respective pages, the teacher can record the accompanying sentences while circulating among the group. For reasons of motivation, each child's page or contribution should be labeled with his name. The books can be easily assembled by using loose-leaf metal rings. The teacher will read the finished book to the class and may ask each child to read his page. After the books are completed, they should be displayed on the library table for independent reading and for children to examine during their free time. Word cards from the group books should be made available on the same table where the books are displayed. Copies of the books can be duplicated for each child. Some group books may be donated to the school library. The group books can be used for word study as children select words to be added to the class word bank(s) and as individual children identify known words to be added to their personal banks.

For children who are having difficulty with reading in the content areas of science and social studies, the language procedures for pupil-composed materials can be particularly useful. For example, with a particular topic, the teacher could provide the stimulus for learning by a field trip, pictures, a film strip, or by conducting an experiment. The next step would be oral discussion of the experiences and content. Pupils' ideas are recorded and the content is then in their language and is available as reading material. As additional experiences occur, more pupil-composed material will be developed. In effect, pupils create their own texts.

In motivating experience stories with children of limited experience backgrounds, a teacher may direct the discussion more specifically and may narrow the topic considerably. For example, a simple question which relates to something very concrete and personal within the realm of children's experiences can be used. Questions such as the following could be asked:

What is your name?
What things are green (red, yellow, etc.)?
Where do you live?
Who is your friend?
What do you like to do?
Who is in your family?
How old are you?
What do you like to eat?
What color is your shirt?
What did you see on your way to school?

Many additional questions of this nature could be posed, and in many cases, a one sentence answer could constitute the entire individual contribution to a class book in the beginning stages. In using this technique, the teacher must be careful not to limit children's talking to this type of expression but should realize that this technique can be a way of starting to put children's speech into written form.

Personal stories, bulletin board displays, group books, and group charts could be developed in connection with each of the topics suggested previously.

A Group Book   A Group Chart   A Bulletin Board Display

Some words of caution may be in order here. Experience stories can be fresh and original, but they can also be trite and stilted. The secret behind the production of imaginative material lies in the teacher's ability to free children to express themselves naturally. With a list of suggested story topics there is the danger that the list may not relate to the interests of a particular group of children. Controlling or predetermining the content is not congruent with the language experience philosophy.

There is a danger, too, that experience stories can become stale and dull for children. If too much repetition occurs, then the productions may lose their appeal. Perhaps it is better to write too many stories than to drill too much on each story. Some stories will be less interesting than others; for certain stories the follow-up activities can be minimized. Not every follow-up activity is suggested for every story.

Another danger with language experience reading is that there may not be sufficient repetition of mastery of vocabulary and certain reading skills. The use of follow-up activities for rereading is a way of providing such mastery.

The follow-up activities should be planned carefully so that objectives can be met. For example, if the objective is to have the child to be able to match word, phrase, and letter cards, then the child's demonstration of that behavior should be carefully observed. Certain skill instruction will need to be provided in situations other than the language experience activities.

Summary

Group experience stories, individual experience stories, and group books are the major types of pupil-composed materials in the language experience approach. The procedures for developing these three types of materials are similar since attention is given to motivation, discussion, recording, reading, and follow-up activities for each. The motivation and oral discussion which precede the recording of pupils' thoughts are stressed, and the recording must be in their language. Reading of the material should occur immediately after its creation, and follow-up activities should be provided for extra practice and direct teaching of skills. The focus is on the acceptance of the children's language and on functional and creative aspects of the experience stories in the total classroom program.

Suggested Readings

Armstrong, Mary K. "First Grade Lift-off with Library Books and Lots of Energy," *The Reading Teacher* 27 (May 1974):778–80. A description of first grade language experience activities is the focus of this article. Teachers will find the suggestions for motivating stories and for providing literature experiences helpful.

Askland, Linda C. "Conducting Individual Language Experience Stories," *The Reading Teacher* 27 (November 1973):167–70. This article contains detailed directions for helping aides to work with individual experience stories.

Herrick, Virgil E., and Nerbovig, Marcella *Using Experience Charts with Children*. Columbus, Ohio: Charles E. Merrill Publishing Company, 1964. Detailed instructions for constructing and using experience charts with children are described. The illustrations depicting examples make this a valuable resource for the teacher who is learning how to use experience charts. Many types are discussed with application to various curriculum areas and grade levels.

Lee, Dorris M., and Allen, R. V. *Learning to Read through Experience*. New York: Appleton-Century-Crofts, 1963, pp. 30–73. Lee and Allen describe both the types and uses of experience charts as they explain the place of experience stories in the framework of language experiences in reading.

Stauffer, Russell G. *The Language Experience Approach to the Teaching of Reading*. New York: Harper and Row, Publishers, 1970. In Chapter 2 Stauffer discusses the use of experience stories in beginning reading. Many examples and detailed procedures are included.

chapter four

Writing Creatively in the Language Experience Approach

Creative writing is a natural component of language experience learning since encouraging pupil authorship is a major concern of the language experience approach. A continuous program of written expression should be part of the elementary curriculum. The program should allow for varied experiences that provide the ideas and activities for creative writing. Creative written expression does not begin after children have learned to write or spell; instead, writing is started as part of the pre-reading and beginning reading stages.

Creative writing springs from personal experiences which pupils wish to communicate through written language. In creative writing, responses must be personal and must come from the pupils' lives and experiences. Writing grows from oral language expression; thus, creative writing fits into the language experience sequence of communication, from thinking and speaking to writing and reading. Children cannot write imaginatively unless they have something to say and will not write imaginatively if they feel there are constraints about the acceptability of ideas and form. To teach creative writing, instruction must include experiences and exposure to the writing of others, and the setting must include acceptance as well as motivation.

As children's reading programs become combined ones beyond the initial stages, creative writing provides the means of using pupils' thoughts and spoken language to further language development. As children make the transition from dictated to independently written stories, their stories are used less for developing reading vocabulary and more for fostering creative expression. Creative writing beyond the beginning stage does provide some reading material, making reading and writing personal and functional. The stories, however, are not the main body of reading materials at higher levels. Language study can develop from the original writing of pupils, and the writing experiences themselves can help pupils to put many language arts skills to use. The *use* of creative writing in the language experience approach involves more than the experience of writing itself.

Creative writing is not a separate or isolated activity but an integrated language experience in which children express thoughts, feelings, and experiences through written language. In creative writing, as in the experience stories, the process of communication is of greater importance than the finished product. In developing the children's power to write creatively, the teacher must present the children with opportunities for self-expression and divergent thinking and must provide the stimulation to release creativity as the children communicate their personal ideas through writing. The goals of creative writing experiences are to increase the power of written expression, to develop language awareness, and to provide stimuli and outlets for creativity. Vocabulary development should result from the opportunities to use words through writing. As children read the ideas of others, more experiences become available to them from which to create. The reader will note the interrelatedness of the chapters on vocabulary development, literature, and creative writing since these three types of language experiences are closely tied together, and attention to one area may involve the other areas as well.

In discussing creative writing in the language experience approach, it is necessary to examine how creative writing becomes a part of the total reading and language program. As children talk, as they encode, and as they read, the communication cycle in the language experience approach relies heavily on their writing.

In chapter 3 the focus was on experience stories which are a form of creative writing but which tend to have more teacher direction in the early stages of instruction than does the creative writing beyond the beginning. At the higher levels, the children who have acquired skills in handwriting and spelling can produce their own stories in creative forms. However, at these higher levels children may feel that they must conform to rigid standards or high expectations as to the correctness of form; therefore, they may not feel confident in their ability to be creative or may not feel that their efforts will be praised and accepted. At all levels an atmosphere which encourages, nurtures, and welcomes creative and original expression must be present if children are to grow in their ability to use written language expressively and effectively.

Underlying Principles of Creative Writing

Certain conditions foster creativity in children; others stifle it. Torrance has found that teacher personality and type of classroom environment affect the children's creative performance.[1] In developing an effective instructional program of creative writing, the following principles must be considered.

An atmosphere of acceptance and freedom is essential.   Teachers must believe that each child has the potential to be creative. Climate and the process of self-expression are more important than a polished product. What children write must be accepted and valued by the teacher. Children must feel secure to venture new ideas and unusual thoughts and to experiment with written expression. All children in the elementary school cannot be expected to be gifted writers, and even children who write well will not produce quality writing every time, but all children should feel that their contributions are accepted.

Evaluation of pupils' written expression should be on an individual basis. Creative writing must not be graded.   Burrows writes, "The quality and sincerity of child writing dwindles to nothing if fear and self-consciousness set in."[2] If children feel that set standards must be met each time they write and if their writing is to be graded, their freedom to create is blocked. Myers and Torrance talk of "time to think without being threatened by grades or tyrannized by time."[3] Evaluation occurs as children keep individual folders of stories and note improvements. Teachers may keep individual records of pupils' writing and note the qualities of originality, richness of expression, word quality, organization, and imagination. Occasionally, classes should talk about qualities or characteristics of good writing so that children will have some criteria for individual evaluation.

Children should be free to select their topics and to determine length and form.   Since creative writing is personal, as the child puts down in *his* language what he feels and thinks, he selects the words used and the ideas communicated. When children write, topics should be open-ended with freedom of choice. Children also should have the option of choosing *not* to write.

Instruction in creative writing consists of more than having children record their thoughts in writing.   Time must be spent on motivation, discussion, and sharing as well as on writing. Since children must have ideas and experiences from which to create, the teacher has a responsibility for providing experiences and models which children can draw upon for their own creative efforts. To develop pride of authorship, pupils need to share their writing with others and to have some of their stories and poems included in a class or individual book, a class newspaper, or in a bulletin board display.

---

[1]E. Paul Torrance, *Guiding Creative Talent* (Englewood Cliffs, N.J.: Prentice-Hall, Inc., 1962).

[2]Alvina Burrows, Doris C. Jackson, and Dorothy O. Saunders, *They All Want to Write* (New York: Holt, Rinehart & Winston, Inc., 1964), p. 43.

[3]R. E. Myers and E. Paul Torrance, *Teachers Guide, Invitations to Speaking and Writing Creatively* (Boston: Ginn and Company, 1965), p. v.

Creative writing as defined in this chapter refers to that writing done by a child which is a reflection of his thoughts and experiences expressed in his choice of form and style. In her informative book on children's writing, Burrows makes a distinction between practical and personal writing.[4] Practical writing serves a functional purpose of communicating to others through letters, reports, or memos, and it is basically informative or entertaining. Personal writing, however, is done to please the writer, and not necessarily to enlighten others. Even though practical writing can be creative and can contain some elements of individuality, in this chapter the focus is on creative writing of the imaginative and personal nature.

In practical writing, when materials are designed to be read by others, there is a need for stressing spelling, punctuation, penmanship, and neatness. In the first draft of creative efforts, however, children should not be concerned with set standards. In creative writing experiences the child should express in his language what he feels to be important. It is hoped that through many experiences with written expression children will apply the knowledge of punctuation, capitalization, spelling, and other mechanics of writing.

Conducting Creative Writing Experiences

In planning creative writing experiences, the teacher must consider motivation, oral discussion before the actual recording, writing, the sharing of individual efforts, and, in some cases, subsequent or follow-up activities.

Teachers will find numerous suggestions for motivating creative writing in the supplementary readings cited at the end of this chapter. It should be stressed that one of the teacher's primary obligations in promoting creativity is to provide a supportive environment and to generate ideas and enthusiasm. Some of the proven means for encouraging thought on a particular topic are (1) presenting a children's literature story or poem, (2) showing some appealing pictures, (3) asking stimulating questions, and (4) suggesting imaginative topics. However, regardless of the effectiveness of the motivation or technique used, children often are asked to write before thinking is truly stimulated. Thus, creative writing becomes an assignment instead of a language and thinking experience.

Oral discussions should be held before children are directed to write their ideas. Questions of "How does this look?" "How does it make you feel?" "What can you see, hear, or touch?" What are some interesting words you would want to use to describe what you see, hear, and feel?" stimulate thought. Children can react in an oral situation and can see that their responses are accepted. In the discussion the teacher should make many accepting comments such as, "That's a fine idea; you can use it in your story," or "That's an interesting way to describe what you feel. Can you include that when you write your ideas?" or "That's a sentence with lots of action; your story will probably be an exciting one." With comments of this nature, the children will feel encouraged to ex-

---

[4]Burrows, Jackson, and Saunders, *They All Want to Write*, pp. 2–5.

press their ideas. Another result of the discussion stage should be the realization that many types of stories are acceptable. Even though the motivation and discussion may have concentrated on a single theme, students are encouraged to develop that theme from various angles.

As children write their stories, the teacher can be available for help with words as needed. When a child asks how to spell a word, it is advisable for the teacher to write the word for him to copy. Every teacher is probably familiar with the situation in which a word is spelled orally, and the child asks the teacher to repeat the spelling with the requested words sometimes still incorrect in the child's story. The cards for the requested words can be put in the child's word bank, and the individual banks can be used as references during creative writing. With all the stress frequently put on the mechanics of writing and on the correctness of written work, it is recommended that the motivation for writing not be lessened by reminding children to spell and write correctly immediately before composing their stories. It is suggested that the teacher tell the children they can write about any of the ideas discussed or about something else if they wish. This type of comment emphasizes the open-ended dimension of the topic. Pupil choice must be respected. Generally, if an idea is well presented and appealing to children, they will be content to write about it. However, children should be free to approach any topic in a variety of ways or to write about something else if they choose to do so.

The sharing of creative writing provides a setting for functional listening, speaking, and oral reading. Small groups can be formed for pupils to read their stories to each other, or the teacher can read the stories to the group. Often when the teacher reads very expressively, children are surprised at how much their stories communicate. During the sharing periods, the teacher can comment on the good qualities of the stories mentioned in the oral discussion. Again, the focus is on acceptance and on language awareness stemming from the pupils' existing use of language. Sharing through displays should also be included. Collections of children's stories should be available in the classroom library and reading center, and stories can be taped and available in the listening center.

DESCRIPTION OF A SAMPLE CREATIVE WRITING EXPERIENCE

Background information.   The experience described here occurred in a fifth grade class, and the examples of the children's writing are exactly as they recorded them. In this example, *The Sun Is a Golden Earring* by Natalia Belting[5] was the only material needed other than pencils and paper for writing. In addition to the general objectives of developing creativity through writing and of enjoying literature, the objectives of this lesson were for children to be able:

1. To identify expressive words and phrases in order to develop language awareness;

---

[5]Natalia Belting, *The Sun Is a Golden Earring* (New York: Holt, Rinehart & Winston, Inc., 1962).

2. To write a story or poem using descriptive words;
3. To express their thoughts in written language.

Motivation.   The teacher introduced the book by explaining that *The Sun Is a Golden Earring* is a collection of short myths and legends from around the world about heavenly bodies and weather. These legends were told by ancient peoples to explain phenomena they could not understand.

The title was discussed as a comparison, and the pupils were asked to listen for other comparisons in the book. The teacher wrote these questions: "What words help you see how something looks?" "What words tell how something sounds?" She then read the book aloud without any discussion during the reading.

Discussion.   The teacher asked what comparisons the students noticed and they mentioned: "The sky is a tent roof," "The stars are a woman's necklace," and "The rainbow is a fishing line of the king of the dragons." The questions listed under motivation were discussed.

After talking about the book, the children were asked if they could describe the things in the sky or the kinds of weather. Gradually, pupils began to volunteer ideas. With each suggestion, praise and acceptance were given. Many times the teacher would say "That's an interesting description," or "That's a good word to use to describe the way that looks." The discussion was a warming-up period to help children formulate their ideas and realize that their suggestions would be accepted.

Writing.   Before the children started to write, the teacher reminded them that they had expressed many good ideas which they could use in their stories or descriptions. The topic was open-ended, for it was suggested that they could write a brief explanation of how something in the sky came to be or something about weather or something entirely different if they wished.

As the children wrote, the teacher assisted with words which she wrote on small slips of paper for the children's word banks. In no case did she say, "Remember capital letters and punctuation." As she walked around, she made comments such as, "That's a good idea," "You describe that well," "You're off to a good start. Could you tell a little more how that happened or how it looks?" "That's a different idea," and "Good."

Reading.   Children should decide whether or not their work is to be shared with others. In this lesson, the teacher collected the papers and said, "As I was watching you write, I saw many good stories and I think you would enjoy hearing them. When I come to your paper, will you tell me if I can read your story?" She then proceeded to call each child's name, to read the stories, and to comment favorably on some feature of each child's work. If a child said not to read his, that wish was respected but again a favorable comment was made. Interesting uses of words were noted by the teacher and the children during this sharing session.

Follow-up activities. After the lesson described here, the children copied and illustrated their stories, which were used for a bulletin board display. Some interesting words and phrases were added to the class compilation. (See p. 52.) The book was available for individual reading. In order to provide additional experience with this type of writing, the writing center featured the question, "Can you write a legend about heavenly bodies or about the weather?"

EXAMPLES FROM A FIFTH GRADE CLASS

How an Ordinary God Made Lightning

Once a long time ago a very ordinary God wanted to talk to his friends in the sky. So he decided to go and try to talk to the Rain God. Now this very little meak God had never spoken a word before and wondered what it would be like. He thought for a while before he opened his mouth. He thought it might be like a trumpet or like the birds singing in the trees. But when he opened his mouth he found something very different. He could speak just like any other God but he had something specail. He found he could flash his teeth as he pleased for they were as bright as the Sun God. When He went to show the other Gods they said he must be the lightning God. And to this day when ever the lightning God talks there is lightning.

Lightning

There was an old lady who lives in the heavens. And all year long she would sit and sew. Sometimes she would drop her needle and it would fall and tear the sky. But then the sky was magic and after it was torn it would heal very quickly and that made Lightning.

Rain

Up in the heavens live an old man. All year long he would sit and smoke his pipe. When he was finished smoking he wouud shake the ashes out of his pipe. The ashes would fall to the earth. And this made Rain.

Snow and How It Became

Once there was a woman in the heavens who's husband was a god. One day her husband got up early and forgot to make his bed, so his wife had to make it. So she had to change the sheets and pillowcases. (because he slept on 15 pillows.) She went to shake the 15th pillow, which was the largest, and the seam came apart and the little tiny feathers flew down from the heavens. Now the god's wife had to go down and pick it up. And that is how the snow comes and goes.

The Story of Rain

One day a young and beautiful god was walking a long and saw a little boy pick and trample a beautiful flower. When she saw this she began to weep. Now every time a flower is picked anywhere she begins to weep. Her weeping is the rain.

Thunder and Lightning

Thunder is when the footplayers of both teams have the same score. And when one of the kickers of the team kicked the ball it sounded like thunder and it streeked through the sky like lightning and makes the winning point.

Snow

Snow is like a clean white sheet that has fallen across the United States and all the kids are happy. They take their sleds and other things. Then the one of the old and meanest of all the sun gods took the sheet and wouldn't give it back till next winter.

Thunder, Rain, and, Lightning

One day some angles and some of the gods went bowling. The first angle missed and he started to cry. The next person was a god and he rooled the ball and sparks came and the Bang! all pins fell down the god was so happy the sun came out and the skies were clear again and all the people on earth were happy it stoped thundering, raining and lighting.

How Saturn Got its Rings

Once there was a great Queen who was very mean and she was very gready! She had a very huge chest of rings. In fact she had 100 for every finger. Thoe she was gready she was also as beautiful as the sunrise in the morning coming up over the montains. And she fell in love with a Prince, but he was not gready so he made her give up all her ring but 10 she didn't no what to do with them so she gave them to a planit called Saturn.

Rain

There was a god's wife who was peeling onions and the "fumes" made her cry. We call this rain.

Earth

There was a big turtle that walked in the heavens and one day died and fell into the space which took up the room of the earth and great vines grow and trees grow. Animales and a god lived there. We call it earth.

Hail

Someone from the heavens throwing rocks down to the earth.

The Moon and the Milky Way

Someone poured milk into the moon and it came out the bottom and fell into which we now call the Milky Way. The color white that you still see is the Milk stain which will stay there forever and ever.

How The Clouds Came to Be

The stars are a diamond teakettle and when the gods decide to have tea they boil the tea and steam comes out and forms the clouds.

How Rain, Thunder and Lighting is Caused

There was once a king who was mean and selfish. His palace was on the highest peak in the world. Whe he is mad he walks around and stampes his feet which caues thunder. He is so selfish he drank the all the water in the kingdon spilling haft the water which caues rain. The king's taxes were hight. Lighting was caused by the gold coins droping from his hand when he is counting it.

Thunder is like a stampid of elephants thundering across the heavens the lightning is there tails flashing across the sky.

Thundering

Thundering is two clouds smashing together. An horses feet claping in heaven And two people fighing and sceaming in heaven.

The Sound of a Horse

When a horse goes trotting in the lomesome dark streets, the hoofs sound like a man running from tearer. And when lighting strikes, the horse get's faster and faster intil it sounds like a tribe of Indians having a war party.

How Rain Developed (a story of the gods)

One day when the earth was being formed it was very hot on earth. One day up in the heaven's a God was watering his lawn with a sprinkler The drops that hit the floor went through and some hissed. So they fell on the earth. Some were stuck in the web that separates earth from the heaven. They made the morning dew. Every time the Cheif God wanted rain he would call the man and tell him to turn on the sprinkler to water his lawn. Thats how rain developed

P.S. But of course he gets mean and doesn't turn it on. So we have a drought.

Thunder and Lightning

thunder—when a baseball Maneger and the Umpire are argueing and when a baseball player catches a line drive
lightning—when a baseball player hits a homerun and the ball streaks into the stands

When it rain's

1) When it rain's it's like a water sprinkler coming from the sky.
2) It's like dimes falling out of your pocket's, Like pennies gold and silver.

Thunder

I think thunder is when two mad scientists get angry when there out in the rain and shoot fifty calibre machine guns hit the clouds and the clouds yell.
Fog is from meteors coming close to earth. The used fuel from the fire on them comes into our atmosphere.

How snow looks to me

It is a God poping pop corn. He has a burning fire and pop corn is falling out. Poeple on earth are grabbing it and eating all they want.

Stars

Stars are white cookies that float in the sky. And Stars are big snow flakes.

Clouds

Clouds are smoke that travle under the sky, which is light.

Clouds And How They Were Formed

Clouds are like smoke from a chimney of a house in the heavens or a horse kiking up dust in the heavens.

What horses look like

Horses look like whitecaps on the dark blue sea. When the whitecaps swirl around madly, horses are galloping. When they're calm horses are trotting. Horses are so swift you can barely see their flying manes and tails which look like breezes blowing the green grass.

The Grass

The grass is like a slimy thin green snakes that have grown from the ground.

The procedure described in the preceding example was used again with the book *The Long-Tailed Bear and Other Indian Legends* also by Natalia Belting.[6] The stories in this book are North American Indian tales or "why" stories about animals. The following examples were written after fifth grade children heard "How the Cardinal Got His Red Feathers" taken from this collection.

How the Cat Got His Fur

One day there was only one cat in the world. It belong to a Barber. The cat always stood right under his masters feet. One day the Barber got a customer who had a lot of hair to be cut. First the Barber had to put a very sticky liquid on the man's head. By accident it fell on the cat so the Barber got another jar. He forgot to wipe the mess up and started cutting the man's hair. The cat rolled into the hair and it stuck tightly. That is how the cat got his fur.

How The Horse Got It's Tail And Mane or
How The Horse Got Short Hair

The horse used to have a very long coat. He was shaggier than a English Sheep Dog. It was summer and as hot as a forest fire. The horse was very hot, so he went to the lion and asked him to cut his coat with his teeth. The lion agreed. It was very cool without his long coat. None of his hair grew back except where his mane and tail are. ——The lion was magic and he knew that the horse would be cold in winter, so the horse's hair grows back in winter and he sheds in the summer

A White Rabbit and How it got its fur

A white rabbit it is so white it it looks like some snow has fallen on him. And he ran back to the forest and try to shake it off. but it couldn't come off. And it turn in to fur.

How the Fox got the white tip on his tail

A red fox which was as bright as the sunset was walking through the woods He decided to see "Man's House." So he he went their. "Man" had just finished painted his house snow white. He left the paint on the steps. Fox accidentally dipped the tip of his tail in the paint That's how the fox got his white tip.
P.S. ALL HER babies were born naturlly with white tips.

How the fox got his white tail

The fox was walking though the woods one day. He was very unhappy with his red tail because his red tail was like the red carnidel and the cat would come and jump on them. So he was walking though the wood one day when he saw

---

[6]Natalia Belting, *The Long-Tailed Bear and Other Indian Legends* (Indianapolis: The Bobbs-Merrill Co., Inc., 1961).

a can labled white paint. So he dipped his tail in the paint and he thought that his whole body was white like the saimise cat. He was disapointed when he found out his body wasn't white. He told about it and they thought it looked nice so they dipped theirs in the white paint.

Why Spiders Have Six Legs and Why Some are black

Once there was a spider that had three children so, she had thre legs. She got the other three legs to mined her white washed web and to wash the dishes and answer the telephone. The nexed day her neighbor sent her child over to play. He was going to put black ink all over them He put black ink on the mother and one child but, he ran out of ink so, the others were brown because that was what coler they relly were.

The End

How Our Hair Got its Color

Once apon a time there was a little girl with golden braids, named Audrey.
She was very curious and one day she asked her father why her hair was yellow.
Her father said, "Well, once there was a little girl with tan hair. She didn't like it she said it looked as though someone didn't wash it good enough.
One day her mother said, "Go outside and polish the silver lamp.
While she was polishing it a funny thing happened, smoke rose from it like someone was smoking a pipe inside it. A "jini" appeared and said "You have one wish.
She quickly said "I wish the fur on heads could be as yellow as the buttercups, as brown as the mud that lies on the earth, as black as the blackbirds or as red as the cardinal's wings are.
And to this very day those are still the colors of hair!

OTHER TEACHING SUGGESTIONS

In a continuing program of creative writing, suggestions such as the following are appropriate.
Children can start a collection of the interesting language used in their stories. Using their words *verbatim* is an excellent practice since the children will then realize that they can say things in an expressive manner and that their expressions are valued by the teacher and by their classmates.
For example, in a second grade class, the children discussed what they would do if they had a hundred dollars to spend. In the individual stories written following the discussion, one boy wrote, "If I had a hundred dollars to spend I'd buy a bike so I could ride up and down the hills like the waves coming in fast." This simile was personal for this child who had had experiences at the nearby Chesapeake Bay. The group discussed why the comparison of the bike ride to the waves made the story more interesting than merely stating, "I'd ride up and down the hills." The sentence was placed on a chart labeled "Interesting Language," and other examples were added each time the group wrote stories.

Another example was a description of giving a dog a bath, "His chin had a beard of soap suds." The children in this particular group were highly motivated to express their ideas in interesting ways and enjoyed having their expressions recognized by the total group.

The reading of literature to children every day is a source of input which adds to the background for creativity. Creative writing can follow the reading of certain literature selections. Children need exposure to the ideas of many authors. Discussion of the style, literary devices, and forms of writing can be initiated with literature examples. (See chapter 6.)

Alerting children to the creative writing of children available in commercial publications is also recommended. The books *Miracles*[7] and *The Wind and the Rain,*[8] edited by Richard Lewis, are excellent examples of children's writing in published form. Hall and Gambrell have described a number of publications in which children are the authors.[9] Children frequently react very favorably to these writings of other children.

Collecting the children's writing and duplicating copies of a class book for each child are other means for maintaining interest in writing. Story starters, such as the open-ended sentences suggested in chapter 3, can be helpful material for a writing center or as the focus for a directed lesson. In classrooms where children are comfortable in expressing feelings, a starter such as "I wish" or "I feel" can result in some probing creative expression.

Inviting other classes to hear children read their original stories and poems usually appeals to children.

Arranging attractive displays of the children's stories on bulletin boards and in the classroom reading center demonstrates that children's efforts are valued. Using children's stories for display purposes in the halls and in the school library also promotes interest in writing.

Some schools and school systems have conducted "Young Author's Fairs" in which children's works are displayed along with programs which may feature noted authors of trade books or other topics related to encouragement of children's creative efforts. Humphrey and Redden describe a young authors' project which had as its purpose to stimulate children to write creatively, to give recognition to children who write, and to provide books for other children to read.[10] They reported that the books written by children were very popular with children.

A local author can visit the class to talk about the stages in developing a manuscript. Children can be alerted to the need for proofreading a final copy and to the realization that polished copies come only after considerable rewriting.

For imaginative open-ended ways of stimulating productive thinking and imaginative writing, teachers will want to explore the teacher's guides and

[7]Richard Lewis, comp., *Miracles* (New York: Simon & Schuster, Inc., 1966).

[8]Richard Lewis, comp., *The Wind and the Rain* (New York: Simon & Schuster, Inc., 1968).

[9]MaryAnne Hall and Linda B. Gambrell, "Children as Authors," *Elementary English* 49 (October 1972): 889–93.

[10]Jack W. Humphrey and Sandra R. Redden, "Encouraging Young Authors," *The Reading Teacher* 25 (April 1972): 643–51.

pupil idea books by Myers and Torrance.[11] Open-endedness, pupil involvement, and personal reaction and interpretation are distinctive features of all these materials. The directions and suggestions are helpful but not prescriptive.

SOME WORDS OF CAUTION

Teachers are sometimes alarmed about the lack of quality in children's writing, about the similarity of content in a particular child's stories, or about the tendency of children to imitate other children or a particular book or poem. While a teacher is concerned about these behaviors, the need is to convey an atmosphere of acceptance, to provide stimulation to create in a variety of situations, and to continue to offer exposure to a variety of models. Even though children's stories may not appear unique to adults, the teacher must look for that which is original and new for the child who is writing.

Children should have the opportunity to start over if they decide they do not like a particular story. They should also have the option of rough drafts, and it should be explained to them that frequently a story must be rewritten to make the language and ideas satisfactory. Children should not be forced to write on a particular day if no suggestions appeal to them. Attitude and interest are crucial, and demanding a composition may have many negative results.

Teachers should realize too that while many language experiences will not lead directly to creative writing, discussions of words, exposure to the language of literature, and encouraging reflective and divergent thinking are the foundation for imaginative writing.

Summary

Creative writing experiences contribute to the language experience approach to teaching communication skills. Through the recording of original thoughts in written language, children are creating personal reading materials which can lead to further language study. The teacher's responsibility is to provide an accepting atmosphere and stimulation of the encouragement of pupil writing. A directed creative writing experience includes motivation, oral discussion, recording by children, and in some cases, sharing of individual creative efforts with other children.

Creative writing seeks to encourage the process of expressing thoughts in original and fresh ways, thereby increasing the power to use language. The experience is more important than the product. If creative writing is to be successful, the atmosphere must encourage creativity in all areas. The personality and attitudes of the teacher determine the children's freedom to create.

---

[11]R. E. Myers and E. Paul Torrance, *Invitations to Speaking and Writing Creatively* (Boston: Ginn and Company, 1965); *For Those Who Wonder* (Boston: Ginn and Company, 1966); *Plots, Puzzles and Ploys* (Boston: Ginn and Company, 1966).

Suggested Readings

Applegate, Mauree. *Easy in English.* Evanston, Ill.: Row, Peterson and Company, 1962. Applegate discusses creativity in relation to all of the language arts. As teachers read her book, they will note many suggestions for developing children's power to write creatively.

Burrows, Alvina; Jackson, Doris C.; and Saunders, Dorothy O. *They All Want to Write.* New York: Holt, Rinehart & Winston, 1964. Every teacher who works with creative writing should be familiar with this book which clearly elaborates the philosophy regarding writing experiences. The many examples of children's writing add to the impact of the content.

Hall, MaryAnne, and Gambrell, Linda B. "Children As Authors," *Elementary English* 49 (October 1972): 889–93. The focus of this article is on the use of materials written by children to stimulate creative writing. An annotated bibliography of published material written by children is included.

Hennings, Dorothy Grant, and Grant, Barbara M. *Content and Craft Written Expression in the Elementary School.* Englewood Cliffs, N.J.: Prentice-Hall, Inc., 1973. A wealth of examples of children's work and ideas for teachers embellish the pages of this outstanding volume. Among the strengths of this book is the specificity of the explanations of both ideas for writing and of the acquisition of the tools for clear written communication.

Koch, Kenneth. *Wishes, Lies, and Dreams.* New York: Vintage Books, Chelsea House Publishers, 1970. The many poignant examples of children's poetry collected by this insightful author present convincing evidence that children can write powerfully and expressively.

Petty, Walter T., and Bowen, Mary. *Slithery Snakes and Other Aids to Children's Writing.* New York: Appleton-Century-Crofts, 1967. This paperback book contains both theoretical and practical information for the teacher who is interested in providing a dynamic creative writing program. Numerous topics for writing are suggested, and examples of children's work are included.

Walter, Nina Willis. *Let Them Write Poetry.* New York: Holt, Rinehart & Winston, 1964. Walter's paperback book explores poetry writing from the kindergarten through high school. Examples of children's writing are included, and the examples for developing awareness of poetic expression, of imagery, and of word quality are particularly well described.

Wolsch, Robert A. *Poetic Composition through the Grades.* New York: Teachers College Press, Columbia University, 1970. This book can help teachers to recognize the depth of expression in children's writing which may go undiscovered and untapped in some classrooms. Many suggestions are offered for motivating children to write.

Yamamoto, Kaoru. *Experimental Scoring Manuals for Minnesota Tests of Creative Thinking and Writing.* Kent, Ohio: Bureau of Educational Research, Kent State University, May 1964, pp. 102–158. A scoring guide for evaluating the "creativity" of imaginative stories written by children in grades 3–6. Six categories of criteria (organization, sensitivity, originality, imagination, psychological insight, richness of expression) are discussed and illustrative examples are included.

chapter five

Vocabulary Development in the Language Experience Approach

"What are words?
Words are how what you think inside comes out
And how to remember what you might forget about." [1]

To say we speak, listen, read, and write with words seems to be stating an all too obvious fact. Even so, is it not also essential to provide planned, directed experiences for developing children's facility with words? To give experience form and substance, children need tools or words for translating events into language. A command of vocabulary is a necessity for conveying and receiving thoughts, feelings, and emotions. If children are to be equipped to put their thoughts into speech or writing and to understand the thoughts of speakers and authors, they must be equipped with the word knowledge these language tasks require.

Extending children's word meanings presents a major focus of instruction in developing the facility to communicate in both spoken and written language. The goals of such instruction are to increase the stock of words used by individuals in their listening, speaking, reading, and writing, to promote awareness of

[1] From Paul Rand and Ann Rand, *Sparkle and Spin* (New York: Harcourt Brace Jovanovich, Inc., 1957).

fine shades of meaning, and to develop an attitude of interest in words. Applegate shows the results of these goals in an anecdote about a fourth grader who told his teacher: "Why, we don't have to be just *mad* anymore. We've learned new words, and now we can be *angry, frustrated, irritated, or furious.*"[2]

Word knowledge has been found to be one of the most significant factors in reading comprehension, while a limited vocabulary presents an obstacle to effective comprehension in reading.[3] The more fluent a child is in oral vocabulary, the greater his resources for associating meaning with printed words. Davis reports that one of the major obligations in teaching comprehension is to make pupils familiar with the meanings of as many words as possible.[4] However, word study should be done in meaningful context within sentence patterns. The language experience approach provides this meaningful context.

In building children's vocabularies, attention must be directed to increasing each of the four types of vocabulary (listening, speaking, reading, and writing). Increased understanding of words in one facet of the language arts should add to understanding in the other facets. In fact, the language experience approach with its integration of the expressive and receptive facets of language provides experiences which contribute to vocabulary development in all areas.

A basic distinction of vocabulary study in the language experience approach is that *the language study stems from the children's oral and written language expression.* In other words, instead of starting with a list of words or passages from language arts textbooks as examples for study, the words selected originate in the children's speech, in their stories, and in their word banks. Word power will grow as children encounter situations in which they need to communicate. In word study, as in all aspects of language experience learning, practical application is the base from which language develops. John Holt states that, "What we have to recognize is . . . that it is the effort to use words well, to say what he wants to say, to people whom he trusts, and wants to reach and move, that alone will teach a young person to use words better."[5]

Research supports the importance of personal meaning and motivation in vocabulary learning. Olson and Pau found that children required significantly fewer trials to learn highly emotional words than were required to learn words without strong emotional associations.[6]

Sylvia Ashton-Warner who achieved phenomenal success in working with Maori children of New Zealand called her work with reading vocabulary "key vocabulary" as she made use of personal word files. She communicates the necessity for personal involvement in the learning as she describes the child

---

[2]Mauree Applegate, *Easy in English* (Evanston, Ill.: Row, Peterson and Company, 1962), p. 29.

[3]Frederick Davis, "Research in Comprehension in Reading," *Reading Research Quarterly* 3(Summer 1968):508.

[4]Ibid., p. 543.

[5]John Holt, "Introduction" in Herbert Kohl, *Teaching the "Unteachable"* (New York: The New York Review, 1966), p. 9.

[6]David R. Olson and A. S. Pau, "Emotionally Loaded Words and the Acquisition of a Sight Vocabulary," *Journal of Educational Psychology* 57(June 1966):174–78.

who stalled for months on the words *come, look, and* and then learned *police, butcher knife, kill, gaol, hand,* and *fire engine* in four minutes in response to the question of what he was afraid of.[7] The *words he wanted to learn* were used to teach him to read. The high impact of the language experience content can affect the learning of reading vocabulary and thus offset the lack of systematic repetition.

Henderson, Estes, and Stonecash reported that children instructed in a language experience approach do acquire sight vocabulary and that the number of words learned compares favorably with the words introduced in basal readers.[8] These researchers also reported that the high frequency function words of the language were frequently present in children's word banks.

Constant extension of the reading vocabulary is a goal of all reading programs at all levels. Language experience reading programs must give attention to the acquisition of a reading vocabulary, although one characteristic of language experience materials is the lack of a controlled vocabulary. Because of the lack of vocabulary control and lack of repetition, teachers may be concerned about students' acquisition of a reading vocabulary. The use of word banks can provide much of the repetition for vocabulary learning in the beginning stages of instruction.

In vocabulary learning in the initial stages of instruction children are exposed to all the written vocabulary used in experience stories. However, teachers should not expect that all of the words written in any story will be learned by those who have participated in creating and reading that story. Each child will identify the words he can read, and those words will go into the individual word bank. In other words, from the first experience stories children will identify one, two, or several words. Gradually, the stock of words known will increase. Also, it is quite common to have children who after a month or two of instruction can identify all the words in the experience stories in their individual folders, even though at the time those stories were written they could only identify two or three words in each story.

What Concepts Do Children Need to Develop about Words?

Not only should children use language effectively with ever-increasing vocabularies, but they should also have an understanding of how words convey meaning in our language. The following list identifies some basic concepts which should be developed with elementary children.

1. *The word is a unit of meaning in the language.* Since word units are such obviously distinct units to adults, it is often assumed that the word units are equally distinct to children. Research studies of beginning

[7]Sylvia Ashton-Warner, *Teacher* (New York: Simon & Schuster, Inc., 1963), p. 43.

[8]Edmund H. Henderson, Thomas H. Estes, and Susan Stonecash, "An Exploratory Study of Word Acquisition among First-Graders at Midyear in a Language-Experience Approach," *Journal of Reading Behavior* 4 (Summer 1972):28.

readers' concept of a word have shown that this concept is not clear to the beginning reader.[9,10] Rystrom notes, "It seems likely that children do not learn what a word is until they have learned to read."[11] In the prereading and beginning reading stages, the concept of word can be shown functionally with language experience stories. (See p. 87.)

2. *Words help express our thoughts.* In order to develop vocabulary as well as any language skill, pupils must see the need for communication in functional settings. Word study should help children understand the interrelationships of speaking, listening, reading, and writing. Pupils should discover that the words they speak can be written and read. They should discover, too, that the words of others can be written and spoken.

3. *The exact meaning of a word is dependent upon the use of the words in context.* Vocabulary study must be in connection with the language patterns in which the words occur. Lefevre, a noted linguist, believes that the sentence, not the word, is the smallest unit of meaning in our language.[12] Goodman puts immense stress on the importance of the syntactical system in reading as he states, "The meaning of a sentence depends on the words or morphemes that compose it, but it is always more than the sum of their meanings."[13] Word study must deal with words used in contextual settings. As children discuss multiple meanings, it is easy to illustrate that the exact meaning of a word cannot be determined apart from the context in which it is used. Developing an awareness of fine shades of meaning and selecting the most appropriate word for the meaning intended must be fostered.

4. *Some meanings can be expressed by more than one word.* Children should be alerted to synonyms as one means of increasing word power. As children work with their individual word boxes and as a group compiles class word banks, there will be many examples of synonyms.

5. *In English there are specific functions of words in the syntactical patterns of the language.* Lefevre identifies two word classifications, full words and empty words. The full words are those which have specific meanings or referents, while empty words are those without a concrete referent. Words such as *the, which,* and *and* are examples of the approximately 300 empty words of English.[14] Children can understand the four word classes noun, verb, adjective, and adverb only as these classes

---

[9]John Downing, "How Children Think about Reading," *The Reading Teacher* 23 (December 1969):217–30.

[10]Nancy J. Meltzer and Robert Herse, "The Boundaries of Written Words as Seen by First Graders," *Journal of Reading Behavior* 1 (Summer 1969):32–40.

[11]Richard Rystrom, "Linguistics and the Teaching of Reading," *Journal of Reading Behavior* 4 (Winter 1972):37.

[12]Carl A. Lefevre, *Linguistics and the Teaching of Reading* (New York: McGraw-Hill Book Company, 1964), p. 6.

[13]Kenneth S. Goodman, "Words and Morphemes in Reading," in *Psycholinguistics and the Teaching of Reading,* ed. Kenneth S. Goodman and James T. Fleming (Newark, Del.: International Reading Association, 1969), p. 27.

[14]Lefevre, *Linguistics,* p. 10.

occur in sentence patterns. Activities with sentence building and the discussion of sentences used in children's writing can illustrate language structure and word functions in sentence patterns. Effective use of vocabulary for the reception and expression of ideas, not the terminology, is the purpose of vocabulary instruction.

Types of Vocabulary

In discussing children's vocabularies, it is again necessary to look at the four dimensions of the language arts. Children have more than one type of vocabulary, and teachers must be concerned with the development of each type. A child's listening vocabulary is composed of those words which he can understand when others use them, although he may not use them in his own speech or recognize them in print. A child has a speaking vocabulary which is composed of those words which he can use in his oral language. As a child learns to read, he acquires a reading vocabulary which is composed of those words which he can recognize in printed form and with which he can associate a meaning. As a child learns to write and spell, he acquires a writing vocabulary. In the early elementary years the listening vocabulary is the largest, the speaking vocabulary is next, then reading, then the writing vocabulary last. The reading vocabulary will surpass the speaking vocabulary in the fourth and fifth grades for those children progressing well in reading.[15]

In the language experience approach, the listening, speaking, reading, and writing vocabularies are extended through activities with group and individual word banks, through literature experiences, and through writing and speaking activities. In the elementary school, concern with reading and writing has overshadowed the teaching of listening and speaking. In vocabulary instruction, stress must be placed on listening and speaking as well as on written language.

Individual Word Banks

Word banks or files kept by individual pupils are one of the major types of material in the language experience approach. An individual word bank is a personal vocabulary file kept by each pupil and used in a variety of ways for promoting vocabulary development and language awareness. A word is put into the word bank after it has been used in an oral or written sentence pattern and after a child is able to read it. In the initial stages of reading instruction, the word banks are used primarily to reinforce the learning of sight vocabulary. As children progress in reading skills, individual word banks can be used as a reference for spelling and writing activities and for oral language discussions about words. In this section, the word banks will be discussed first in relation

---

[15]David H. Russell, *Children Learn to Read* (Boston: Ginn and Company, 1961), p. 266.

to beginning reading instruction and then in relation to other types of language study.

The major functions of the individual word banks are:

1. To serve as a record of the reading vocabulary of individual students;
2. To serve as references for creative writing and spelling;
3. To provide reinforcement through repeated exposure to words;
4. To serve as stimulus words for examples for skill instruction;
5. To provide independent activities with word games, matching activities, sentence building;
6. To provide examples for group language study.

Questions frequently asked by teachers about word banks are: "How is a word bank started?" "What format is the most practical?" "How can words be classified?" "How can the word banks be used for independent activities?" "How can the word banks be used for directed language study?"

The simplest way of starting individual word banks with a class is in connection with either a group experience story or a personal experience story. Any word which a child can identify can be written for his word bank. For example, if the class has composed a group experience story about the classroom pet, a hamster, one child may be able to read the words *hamster* and *brown.* If so, these words will be placed on cards for his word bank. Another child may be able to read the words *hamster, little,* and *eat.* These three words are written for this child's word file. Each child will choose different words, and the teacher should not attempt to have a group of pupils select identical words for mastery.

The above procedure can be followed when working with individual experience stories. The child may be asked to underline the words in his story which he knows. Again, these words are written on cards for his word bank. These word cards will be used for many of the activities described later in this chapter.

Other procedures may be used for starting or adding to the individual word banks. In the beginning stages of reading, pupils' names can be used to arouse curiosity about words. The first word in a child's bank could be his name. As pupils learn to read the names of their classmates, these words could be included in the word banks. Pupils may learn some words from signs and from bulletin board captions around the room. The teacher can explain to the group that if they can read those words, cards will be placed in their banks.

Another source for starting or for adding to the word banks is children's literature. After reading a story to the class the teacher may ask, "What was the most interesting word you heard in this story?" or "What word in the story would you like to know?" One variation of the interesting word idea was used in the compilation of a picture dictionary with a remedial group who selected words for the dictionary from literature examples. After hearing the story *The Tenth Good Thing about Barney*[16] the group selected *fertilizer* and *destination*

---

[16]Judith Viorst, *The Tenth Good Thing about Barney* (New York: Atheneum, 1971).

as words to be included. Typically children are intrigued by words they consider different and ones they think adults may think they won't know.

Some cautions should be noted regarding the above procedures. The teacher should not be in a hurry to have children add too many words to the banks since this may lead to confusion. The rate of learning will differ from pupil to pupil, and the purpose of word banks should not be viewed by pupils as collecting as many words as possible.

Opportunities for rereading and for repeated exposure to words should be provided, especially in the initial stages of instruction. Teachers should not be upset when children occasionally forget a word. In working with commercial reading materials, children will also forget words. Reteaching is in order in both cases. In the language experience approach, reteaching or extra practice can be provided by having the child find the sentence in the story in which he first used the word and by having him read the sentence and underline the word. The child can talk about the meaning of the word and match the card from the bank to the word in the story. One category of words in a bank can be "Words I Need to Work On," and a missed word can be placed in this category. The child can be directed to build a sentence using the forgotten word with cards from the word bank.

Another caution regarding the word banks relates to the selection of words. Children, not the teacher, should select the words they wish to know. However, with some student-composed materials the teacher may ask, "Do you know this word? It is a word you will use in many stories." Some teacher suggestions may be offered, but the selection of the words in the individual word banks remains the child's choice.

Group Word Banks

Word banks can be developed with an entire class or with subgroups within a class. Generally in most classes, there will be many group word banks for various categories of word study. With the group word banks greater attention is placed on general language development and less on reading vocabulary in constrast with individual word banks.

The functions of the group word banks are:

1. To develop language awareness and interest in word study;
2. To focus language study on word categories and functions;
3. To serve as a reference (a type of class dictionary) for word study or as a spelling check when doing independent writing;
4. To provide materials for independent activities with words.

In developing group word banks, discussions and group experience stories will be the main sources of words. The easiest way of initiating group banks with any class is to discuss word categories such as colors, animals, naming words, and so on. For example, in kindergarten or first grade, the first group word file could be an outgrowth of a group experience story. If the pupils have written a story about the colors of the fall leaves, they could be asked to find all the words which name colors. These words could then be written on cards and placed in a box or envelope labeled "color words." If the children have written some chart stories about animals, they could reread these stories and find all the words which name animals and include this classification in a word file. Numerous categories can and should be used.

The meanings of words in the group files should be familiar to pupils, and the words added to the word banks should have been used in the talk and writing of the class so that the first encounter with a word was in a contextual setting. The cards for the group banks can include a sentence definition or a picture with each word. Teachers may wish to number the group experience stories and have a folder of typed copies available in the classroom writing or reading center. This folder should include an envelope of word bank cards which are numbered according to the story in which the words were used. This folder can be useful for independent activities and as a reference for word study.

No single format is satisfactory to all teachers. Regardless of the arrangement, the bank should permit easy reclassification of words, should be organized so children can locate a particular word quickly, and should be styled for easy manipulation during independent study. Having each word on a separate card or slip of paper is recommended. A notebook type of listing does not have the feature of easy manipulation or reclassification. Teachers generally find that oak tag or other relatively heavy paper increases the durability of the word cards. Many teachers find that index cards are easy to use and to file in either a standard size file box or in cardboard boxes.

A card of 1" X 2" is generally adequate for individual use, especially if pupils are going to build sentences at their desks. Also, a small card is more satisfactory for comparison with a word in an individual experience story. During the beginning stages, a teacher may prefer using large word cards and shoe boxes for files.

Providing envelopes for classification into such categories as suggested previously is helpful. Many ways of classifying words should be used and changed throughout the school year.

The group word banks may utilize 4" X 6" or 6" X 8" index cards for visibility by the total group. These can be kept in shoe boxes or large file boxes in the writing center. Again, envelopes for classification are useful, and as the files expand beyond the first grade level, a separate box can be used for each category. For example, there may be a group word bank of synonyms, another of antonyms, another for words with multiple meanings, another for descriptive words, and another for interesting language expressions, word pictures, and similes or metaphors.

Activities with Word Banks

One of the major advantages of the word banks for language study is their adaptability to many types of activities. The classification activity, which is one of the most valuable, can begin very early in the reading and language arts instruction by varying the level and categories according to the children's maturity. Perhaps the simplest means of classification is by alphabetical order. While this is a useful and practical means of locating words easily, the classification of words should not be limited to filing entries in alphabetical order. Language study will be much more appropriate if children study word qualities, definitions, and functions.

As an example of introducing the classification of words at the beginning reading level, a teacher could ask a small group of children to bring their word banks to the reading table and find words which name things. These words could then be examined for those which name people, food, or animals. Another time children could be directed to find all the words which are action or descriptive words. The labeling of nouns, verbs, and other parts of speech is unimportant. What is important is that the children understand how words function in a sentence context to convey meaning and that children constantly increase their word power.

Word banks can lead to the discussions of word categories and then to the development and extension of each category. The teacher can ask the pupils to find the most interesting words in their banks and tell why a particular word is interesting to them. In one first grade class, a child volunteered *glitter* and *sparkle* as the most interesting words. These words had been used in a story describing a Halloween costume. Another child said that *diesel engine* and *blast-off* were the most interesting words. The practice of identifying interesting words can contribute considerably to language awareness.

Children will be introduced to many types of classification as they progress in reading, and teachers will find word banks extremely useful for working with multiple meanings, synonyms, antonyms, homonyms, and other categories. A classification for a particular word should change as the children realize that a particular word may fit in a number of categories depending upon its use in context.

Word banks can be used for sentence building activities as a child or a group of children combine the words in different patterns. The word banks can provide the basis for work with kernel sentences and their extension with additional words. For example, two words such as "Boy jumped" or "Cat ate" can be selected from a bank and the children can be asked to find words which might describe the boy or the cat, words which tell how the boy jumped or what the cat ate. Children can select two words for kernel sentences and ask their classmates to add to the original sentence. When this activity uses the word banks, children are working with *their* language as they extend their knowledge of how words function in sentence patterns.

Word banks are practical for independent reading and language activities. Children can work in pairs or teams as they read each other's words and stories or as they build sentences with the word cards. Some children may want to compile individual dictionaries by writing definitions for the words in their banks.

Children should be encouraged to refer to both the individual and group word banks when doing creative writing. Writing can be motivated by having children select words from the bank to make an interesting title, and then they can write a story for that title. In connection with the study of word categories, children could write a story using as many words of a particular category as possible.

In the classroom writing center, described in chapter 9, word banks should be available for reference for independent writing and independent language study.

Possibilities for group word banks include the following:

Descriptive words	Compound words
Naming words	Words for said
Action words	Words with prefixes
Interesting words	Words with suffixes
Words for sounds	Synonyms
Words for colors	Homonyms
Words for animals	Science words
Opposites	Three-syllable words
Words with more than one	Four-syllable words
meaning	Sports words
Social studies words	Words for feelings

Other Activities for Word Study

Pupils in the intermediate grades can extend and deepen their study of words by probing into the origins of words. Perhaps the class can keep banks of words with interesting origins. Dictionary study can be helpful with this activity as students are alerted to the information about word origins to be found in a dictionary. The brief pamphlet *Pageant of Words*[17] has a number of suggestions for studying word origins and includes the names of appropriate trade books related to word study.

In Other Words is the title of both a beginning and an intermediate thesaurus designed for elementary students.[18,19] These two books can be valuable for developing children's vocabularies as well as adding to their interest in words.

A notebook could be kept on the writing center table or in the reading center for pupil use in recording interesting words found in their independent reading. They can also keep personal lists of these words.

Activities with literature and creative writing also promote vocabulary growth, and the reader is directed to chapters 4 and 6 for other ideas relating to vocabulary.

---

[17]*Pageant of Words* (Glenview, Ill.: Scott, Foresman and Company, 1966).

[18]W. Cabell Greet, William A. Jenkins, and Andrew Schiller, *In Other Words: A Beginning Thesaurus* (Glenview, Ill.: Scott, Foresman and Company, 1968).

[19]W. Cabell Greet, William A. Jenkins, and Andrew Schiller, *In Other Words: A Junior Thesaurus* (Glenview, Ill.: Scott, Foresman and Company, 1969).

Summary

Increasing children's listening, speaking, reading, and writing vocabularies receives major attention in the language experience approach. Opportunities to use words in personal communication situations in speaking and writing provide an excellent means for developing word power. In the language experience approach, many opportunities for discussion of words will occur, and developing an awareness of words should be a continuing goal. In vocabulary development, as in other concerns in the language experience approach, the three characteristics of pupil-composed materials, the interrelationships of all the language arts, and the lack of vocabulary control are apparent.

Through language experience activities children should discover many ways of using words for communication. Individual and group word banks constitute a major tool for vocabulary study as they are used as a record of words learned and as materials for numerous other language activities. The teacher's responsibility is to provide the setting and the stimuli for word study growing from the child's own language.

Suggested Readings

Applegate, Mauree. *Easy in English.* Evanston, Ill.: Row, Peterson and Company, 1962, Chapter 2. Applegate conveys the message of the chapter title, "Words Make the Difference" perceptively and includes activities for extending vocabulary in creative ways.

Ashton-Warner, Sylvia. *Teacher.* New York: Simon & Schuster, Inc., 1963. The description of the "key vocabulary" in teaching reading shows the use of individual word files for vocabulary. The reader will note the emotional impact of the words selected by Mrs. Ashton-Warner's pupils.

Glaus, Marlene. *From Thoughts to Words.* Champaign, Ill.: National Council of Teachers of English, 1965. This paperback book is a collection of ideas for the classroom teacher who wants to combine creativity and language expression.

Tiedt, Iris M., and Tiedt, Sidney W. *Contemporary English in the Elementary School.* Boston: Allyn & Bacon, Inc., 1967, Chapter 3. The chapter on word study contains many activities which can be utilized for developing an interest in word study.

Wilson, Robert M., and Hall, MaryAnne. *Reading and the Elementary School Child.* New York: Van Nostrand Reinhold, 1972, Chapter 6. Developing children's reading vocabulary is the topic of chapter 6 in this textbook on the teaching of reading.

chapter six

Literature as a Language Experience

Literature as a language experience presents opportunities for developing children's language facility in personal, communicative, creative, and functional ways. The place of literature in an elementary reading program is generally accepted as being of utmost significance in promoting pleasurable experiences with reading, thereby contributing to the development of a permanent interest in and favorable attitudes toward reading. The values of literature for entertainment, for extending experience backgrounds, and for developing self-understanding and understanding of others have been well-elaborated by a number of authorities on children's literature.[1,2,3] However, the contribution of literature as a language enriching experience needs greater attention than it currently receives in many classrooms. The freshness and originality of language in children's literature is one of its unique qualities that no other materials or curriculum experiences can offer.

Literature is a *personal* language experience since children respond to stories in individual ways and express their reactions to characters, plots, and themes in terms of their individual

[1]May Hill Arbuthnot and Zena Sutherland, *Children and Books*, 4th Ed. (Chicago: Scott, Foresman and Company, 1972).

[2]Charlotte S. Huck and Doris Y. Kuhn, *Children's Literature in the Elementary School* (New York: Holt, Rinehart & Winston, Inc., 1968).

[3]Leland B. Jacobs, "Children's Experiences with Literature," in *Children and the Language Arts,* ed. Virgil Herrick and Leland B. Jacobs (Englewood Cliffs, N.J.: Prentice-Hall, Inc., 1955), pp. 192–217.

backgrounds. In encouraging divergent reactions to stories read to children and to those which they read for themselves, questions such as, "How did *you* feel?" "What would *you* have done?" "What did this story make *you* think of?" will permit and encourage a variety of responses.

Literature is a *communicative* language experience because children use the receptive language skills of listening and reading in order to absorb ideas. Through discussion of literature and writing about literature, the expressive facets of the language arts are employed.

Literature is a *creative* language experience when it serves as a stimulus for creative thinking and leads to the production of creative stories and poems by children.

Literature is a *functional* language experience since children clearly perceive a purpose to activities with literature and since with these activities listening, speaking, reading, and writing are related to content of high interest and meaning. The creative, personal, and communicative attributes contribute to the purposefulness of the literature experiences.

The value of literature in enriching language backgrounds is supported by the research of Carol Chomsky.[4] In a study of children's linguistic development, she found that for children who had been read to and/or who had read independently the stage of linguistic development was higher than for children who had not had the exposure to literature. Fasick reported that children's literature materials for preschoolers use a far wider range of syntactic patterns than do children's television programs.[5] She advocates the use of literature for development of children's language readiness.

The theme of this chapter is the interrelatedness of language experiences and literature. At all levels in the elementary school, there is a place for experiences with literature which expand vocabulary, which build awareness of writing styles, and which stimulate creative writing. Questions to be examined include: How can literature be used to develop communication skills? How can literature be used to promote vocabulary growth? How can literature be used to develop awareness of styles of writing? How can children's literature be used in the language experience framework of going from speech to recording to reading as pupils create reading materials?

Throughout the chapter, books which are especially applicable in relating literature to other language experiences are cited. The reader will also note that in the chapter on vocabulary development and creative writing, references are also made to literature since these three topics are closely interwoven.

The Teacher's Role

The teacher must provide the time, the motivation, and the materials for children to explore the possibilities of developing language awareness through

---

[4]Carol Chomsky, "Stages in Language Development and Reading Exposure," *Harvard Educational Review* 42 (February 1972): 1–33.

[5]Adele M. Fasick, "Television Language and Book Language," *Elementary English* 50 (January 1973): 125–32.

literature. In a study of children's reading preferences and habits, Helen Huus found that the adults in the environment were a significant factor affecting interest in reading.[6] As the significant adult in the school environment, the teacher must provide the model of valuing literature.

In another source, Hall commented,

> With the growth of school libraries, the inclusion of librarians as part of elementary school faculties, and the increase in the quantity of books available on a range of levels and interests, teachers have more resources than ever before on which to draw in developing dynamic literature programs. However, the resources themselves cannot produce excellent reading programs; teachers must actively draw upon these resources as they put a program into operation.[7]

A survey of the experiences with literature provided by cooperating teachers who were working with student teachers showed that the experiences with literature in many classrooms were limited indeed.[8] Creative experiences were particularly sparse.

Experiences with literature are essential in any good reading program, and in all classrooms the following activities and/or facilities should be included:

1. The daily reading aloud of a children's literature selection by the teacher.
2. A classroom library corner or table where books are displayed attractively and changed frequently.
3. Opportunities for children to explore books as an independent activity.
4. Regularly scheduled time for independent reading.
5. Opportunities for individuals to use the school library as needed, by having open access to it as well having regularly scheduled library periods.
6. Creative activities related to literature (art, drama, creative writing).

In addition to the previously suggested types of experiences the teacher must offer activities with literature which contribute directly to the language experience reading program.

The major purpose in reading literature to children and in encouraging personal reading is to have them enjoy stories. Never should the enjoyment be overlooked as literature is used to contribute to the total language program in some of the ways discussed in this chapter. However, it cannot be assumed that children will become aware of writing styles or of the creative use of language without some direct guidance by the teacher.

---

[6]Helen Huus, "Interpreting Research in Children's Literature," in *Children, Books and Reading, Perspectives in Reading No. 3* (Newark, Delaware: International Reading Association, 1964), p. 127.

[7]MaryAnne Hall, "Literature Experiences Provided by Cooperating Teachers," *The Reading Teacher* 24 (February 1971): 431, 465.

[8]Ibid.

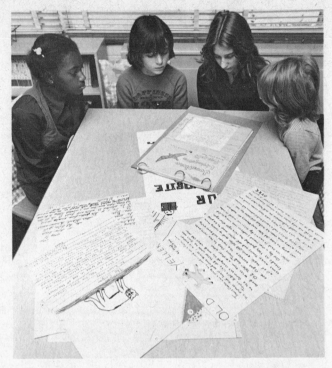

The teacher's responsibilities include knowing many books, developing some techniques for alerting children to language through literature, and providing opportunities for children to use models from literature to express their own ideas in spoken and written language.

How Can Literature Stimulate
Language Awareness?

Language quality is one of the hallmarks of good literature. One of the reasons literature belongs in the elementary curriculum is simply that it is *imaginative language.* Jacobs talks about "colorful, tongue-tickling words and neatly turned phrases" which are a part of storytelling.[9] Through literature, children can experience examples of the creative use of language in a very natural informal way. It is hoped that through exposure to the language of literature children will extend their ability to use language expressively. Exposure to models of original and creative expression by gifted authors is essential if real language awareness and power is to develop in the elementary years. In using literature with children, the intent is for them both to hear and read the best that has been written and to express their own thoughts and ideas. During the early school years, when children's reading skills are minimal, hearing

[9]Jacobs, "Children's Experiences with Literature," p. 198.

literature read aloud is their major exposure to the imaginative use of language. Children's literature materials can serve as a motivation for the creation of pupil-composed materials and can help to lead pupils from spoken language to written language.

Although children will have more experiences with prose literature than with poetry, poetry also can stimulate language awareness and creative responses in children. The imagery, the figurative language, and the brevity of thought can add to the appeal of this branch of literature. Interest, enjoyment, appreciation, and a love for poetry can be nurtured by reading many examples aloud. Teachers should be familiar with anthologies and should develop personal anthologies of their own favorites. They can seek to build an awareness of mood, of visual and auditory imagery, and emotional responses through exposure to poetry. In the following sections on creative writing, vocabulary development, and author's style, examples are drawn from both prose and poetry. The same methodology can be used with each.

How Can Literature Lead to Creative Writing?

One of the major applications of literature in the total language curriculum is as an impetus for creative writing. Through the awareness of language, development of vocabulary, and understanding of style, the tools for personal writing are acquired.

If children are expected to write creatively, should they not be provided exposure to and awareness of the creative use of language and the thoughts of other authors? The input of ideas and of expressive language must be a part of any children's program which seeks to develop the power to communicate in both spoken and written language. The input of ideas through literature is vital if children are going to have a reservoir of knowledge for their own creativity.

As pupils hear and read models of prose and types of poetry, they can be stimulated to write their own stories and poems. For example, fables, tall tales, and haiku are excellent models. Examples of haiku poetry can be found in *Cricket Songs* by Harry Behn[10] and *In a Spring Garden* by Richard Lewis.[11] As in all creative writing, the thought is more important than the form. In haiku poetry the seventeen syllable form can be discussed, but attention should be given to the thoughts expressed instead of to the number of syllables included.

Children's literature can lead to many types of writing about books in addition to the creative formulation of stories and poems. The following are suggested as ways for children to share independent reading with each other through writing.

Written book reports of a routine type are not in harmony with the personal, communicative, creative, and functional philosophy of the language experience approach. However, certain types of writing about books should be encouraged.

---

[10]Harry Behn, comp., *Cricket Songs* (New York: Harcourt, Brace & World, Inc., 1964).

[11]Richard Lewis, comp., *In a Spring Garden* (New York: The Dial Press, Inc., 1965).

Children can be introduced to book reviews through newspapers and periodicals and should experiment with this style of writing. They can try writing personal reviews of their favorite books to interest others in a particular book. Book reviews can be featured in the class newspaper or collected and displayed in the classroom reading corner.

Children can write about and to their favorite authors, and they can share their writing about books in small interest groups and with members of other classes. Character sketches and descriptions for book jackets are other types of writing about books.

In each type of writing, the teacher should first introduce a model to the children. For example, in working with the writing of book jacket descriptions, the teacher could read the children the blurbs from several familiar jackets, and the class could compose together a description for another jacket. Then the children could write individual blurbs to interest other children in the book.

For young children, literature can lead to the creation of group experience charts, individual experience stories, and group books discussed in chapter 3. A group book of pages describing children's reactions to favorite stories could be used with kindergarten and first grade children as they dictate their comments.

At the primary grade levels, reading a story aloud to children can be the stimulus for a group to dictate stories about a similar topic. For example, if children listen to *Swimmy* by Leo Lionni,[12] they could write stories about fish or after hearing *Rufus* by Tomi Ungerer,[13] they could dictate stories about bats. Among the other easy picture-story books which seem to get enthusiastic response for individual stories are *Harry, the Dirty Dog*[14] and the other Harry books by Gene Zion; *Crictor*[15] by Tomi Ungerer; *Danny the Dinosaur*[16] and *Sammy the Seal*[17] by Syd Hoff; *Lyle, Lyle, Crocodile*[18] by Bernard Waber.

Hearing a story read aloud can lead to the writing of a group experience story as the children dictate their reactions to a story or write a summary of the plot.

[12]Leo Lionni, *Swimmy* (New York: Pantheon Books, Inc., 1963).
[13]Tomi Ungerer, *Rufus* (New York: Harper & Row, Publishers, 1961).
[14]Gene Zion, *Harry, the Dirty Dog* (New York; Harper and Row, 1956).
[15]Tomi Ungerer, *Crictor* (New York: Harper and Row, 1958).
[16]Syd Hoff, *Danny the Dinosaur* (New York: Harper and Row, 1958).
[17]Syd Hoff, *Sammy the Seal* (New York: Harper and Row, 1959).
[18]Bernard Waber, *Lyle, Lyle, Crocodile* (Boston: Houghton Mifflin Company, 1965).

The chart could be made to interest another class in a book.

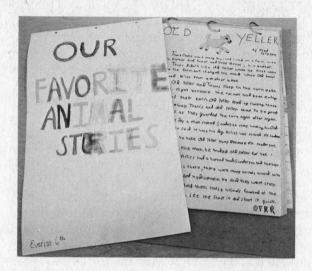

How Can Literature Develop Awareness of Writing Styles?

Style is the quality which makes a piece of writing distinctive and individual. Arbuthnot describes style as "... difficult to define, a quality of which children are unconscious and yet one to which they respond as surely as they respond to a smile."[19] Exposure to various writing styles in literature develops the concept of adapting language to one's ideas which is basic to the goal of helping children to use language more effectively.

In analyzing style, children should be alerted to certain techniques used by writers. The introduction of these techniques can best be illustrated by their occurrence in literature. Studying authors' styles should be carried over to pupils' writing by providing numerous experiences for writing in different moods or for employing different techniques.

Petty and Bowen identify personification, onomatopoeia, alliteration, and internal rhyme as devices which can be easily learned and applied by elementary pupils.[20] Children need not learn the technical names for these techniques but should recognize them when they occur in literature and use them in their own writing.

Personification can be pointed out to young children as they recognize the human characteristics attributed to nonhuman objects in stories like *Mike Mul-*

[19]May Hill Arbuthnot, *Children and Books*, 3d Ed. (Chicago: Scott, Foresman and Company, 1964), p. 18.

[20]Walter T. Petty and Mary E. Bowen, *Slithery Snakes and Other Aids to Children's Writing* (New York: Appleton-Century-Crofts, 1967), pp. 64–70.

ligan and His Steam Shovel[21] and *The Little House,*[22] both by Virginia Burton, and *Little Toot,*[23] *Loopy,*[24] and *Hercules*[25] by Hardy Gramatky. Many other examples of personification exist in children's literature selections. Pupils can be asked to write stories using personification.

In a clinic situation with remedial readers, the grab bag technique has been used to have children experiment with personification. A number of objects are placed in the grab bag and the children are asked to pick one and then write a story beginning with "I am. . . ." Teachers can ask children to compose a story with an object as the main character.

As appropriate examples occur in the poetry read to children, the teacher may comment on the auditory qualities which make particular poems distinctive. Comments such as, "When you write a poem, you might want to use several words which begin alike in a line," or "You might want to try to find words which sound like the idea the word represents," are good examples.

In alerting children to the mood of stories, serious and light stories on the same topic can be read to children for contrast. Children can also identify the words used by an author to create a certain mood. For example, children could compare the mystical mood in *Where Does the Butterfly Go When It Rains?* by May Garelick[26] with the factual descriptions in *Rain Drop Splash* by Alvin Tresselt.[27] Children at upper grade levels can discuss the differences in mood between various books read in their independent study.

The concern is not to develop set techniques or styles for pupils but, through exposure and discussion, to have children realize that style changes according to the content, the purpose of the writing, the mood, and the author. Children should grasp the concept that different authors have different styles just as in class they have different styles. Teachers can encourage children to experiment in their writing by accepting their language, by giving them opportunities to discuss styles of writing in literature examples, and by providing situations for them to employ different styles and techniques in their personal writing.

How Can Literature Contribute to the Development of Vocabulary?

The fact that continued exposure to the language of others results in the development of speaking vocabulary is well-documented by studies of the acquisition of oral language in the young child as he learns to speak from hearing

---

[21]Virginia Burton, *Mike Mulligan and His Steam Shovel* (Boston: Houghton Mifflin Company, 1939).

[22]Virginia Burton, *The Little House* (Boston: Houghton Mifflin Company, 1942).

[23]Hardy Gramatky, *Little Toot* (New York: G. P. Putnam's Sons, 1939).

[24]Hardy Gramatky, *Loopy* (New York: G. P. Putnam's Sons, 1939).

[25]Hardy Gramatky, *Hercules* (New York: G. P. Putnam's Sons, 1940).

[26]May Garelick, *Where Does the Butterfly Go When It Rains?* (New York: William R. Scott, Inc., 1963).

[27]Alvin Tresselt, *Rain Drop Splash* (New York: Lothrop, Lee & Shepard Co., Inc., 1946).

the language of those in his environment. Exposure to the words of literature also adds to a child's vocabulary development. However, in addition to the informal exposure offered by literature, some steps can be taken by teachers to alert children to new words or interesting language descriptions. Teachers must seek to reinforce the informal exposure and to consciously build language awareness.

TECHNIQUES FOR PROMOTING VOCABULARY DEVELOPMENT THROUGH LITERATURE

A chart of interesting words, descriptive phrases, and word pictures from literature can be kept. The teacher must initiate the discussion of language usage if awareness of language is to ensue. Books provide one of the best sources for stretching the imagination and expanding vocabulary. As children hear new stories and poems, they have an opportunity for assimilating new words into their listening and speaking vocabularies. The teacher's responsibility is to alert children before a story is read to listen for the interesting way an author describes a particular person or object, for all the words which describe a person's action, for all the words which describe sounds, and so forth.

A chart such as the following could be kept:

Interesting Language from Books

from *Listen, Rabbit**   "the rain was weeping down the eye of the window pane"

Word Pictures

from *Swimmy†*   "a lobster who moved about like a water moving machine"

---

*Aileen Fisher, *Listen, Rabbit* (New York: Crowell Collier & Macmillan, Inc., 1965).
†Lionni, *Swimmy.*

After reading a story to children, a teacher may ask, "What did you notice about the word_____?" "What did it mean?" "How did the author use that word?" "Do you know any other words which he could have used which mean the same thing?" (It is better not to interrupt a story to explain a word or concept; explanations should occur either before or after the reading.)

The teacher may ask, "What was the most interesting or new word you heard in that story?" When one first grader was asked this question after listening to *The Camel Who Took a Walk* by Jack Tworkov,[28] he replied, "Flabbergasted." A notebook could be kept on the writing center table or in the reading center for additional examples from independent reading.

[28]Jack Tworkov, *The Camel Who Took a Walk* (New York: E. P. Dutton & Co., Inc., 1951).

After reading a story, the teacher can ask, "What kind of person was_____?" or "How did_____feel when_____?" Words such as *greedy, selfish, troublesome, frightened, unpleasant, understanding, sympathetic,* and *optimistic* might be discussed and added to the class word banks.

Children's literature materials which are directly related to vocabulary study are: *Sparkle and Spin* by Ann and Paul Rand,[29] *Words, Words, Words* by Mary O'Neill,[30] *A Hole Is to Dig* by Ruth Krauss,[31] and *Ounce, Dice, Trice* by Alistair Reid.[32]

Awareness of similes and metaphors can be begun even while children are in the prereading stage as they hear stories read aloud. The book *Swimmy* contains many examples of the interesting use of language through comparisons. Children can be asked to listen for how the lobster moved ("like a water-moving machine") or how the underwater flowers, the sea anemones, looked ("like pink palm trees swaying in the wind").[33] *The Sun Is a Golden Earring,*[34] mentioned in chapter 4, contains excellent examples of similes and metaphors. This terminology is unimportant for children in the elementary level. However, the ability to use comparisons to communicate clearly, imaginatively, and expressively must be developed. The poem "Cliche" in *It Doesn't Always Have to Rhyme* by Eve Merriam,[35] is excellent for having pupils identify comparisons. Children can extend the poem's idea to their own writing as they work with, "As warm as_____; as quiet as_____; as soft as_____; as quick as_____." Alvin Tresselt's *How Far Is Far?*[36] is another book that contains many imaginative descriptions which can be used to motivate children's writing.

Summary

Children's literature plays an important part throughout the language experience program in reading. Trade books of many types should be used to enrich the language and experience backgrounds of the pupils. Books can help to expand the reading and speaking vocabularies, to develop concepts, to provide training in purposeful listening as well as to develop the idea that reading is a pleasurable experience. Literature can add to a child's ability to use and understand language and to formulate in words what he sees, hears, feels, thinks, and imagines.

Literature is a language experience, but it is the teacher's responsibility to awaken the children's sensitivity to the language of literature. In so doing, the

[29]Paul Rand and Ann Rand, *Sparkle and Spin* (New York: Harcourt Brace Jovanovich, Inc., 1957).

[30]Mary O'Neill, *Words, Words, Words* (New York: Doubleday & Company, Inc., 1966).

[31]Ruth Krauss, *A Hole Is to Dig* (New York: Harper & Row, Publishers, 1952).

[32]Alistair Reid, *Ounce, Dice, Trice* (Boston: Little, Brown and Company, 1958).

[33]Lionni, *Swimmy.*

[34]Natalia Belting, *The Sun Is a Golden Earring* (New York: Holt, Rinehart & Winston, Inc., 1962).

[35]Eve Merriam, *It Doesn't Always Have to Rhyme* (New York: Atheneum Publishers, 1966).

[36]Alvin Tresselt, *How Far Is Far?* (New York: Parents' Magazine Press, 1964).

teacher must be aware of the examples of interesting language in children's books, must call the children's attention to these examples in a variety of ways, and must provide the stimulation and opportunities for children to develop their own creativity with language.

Suggested Readings

Arbuthnot, May Hill, and Sutherland, Zena. *Children and Books,* 4th Ed. Chicago: Scott, Foresman and Company, 1972. A basic reference source about children's literature, this book contains much detailed information about types of literature, about authors, and about criteria for evaluating children's books.

Hopkins, Lee Bennett. *Books Are by People.* New York: Citation Press, 1969. Anecdotes about and comments by 104 authors and illustrations of children's books form the substance of this unique publication.

Huck, Charlotte S., and Kuhn, Doris Y. *Children's Literature in the Elementary School.* New York: Holt, Rinehart & Winston, Inc., 1968, Chapters 11, 12, 13. The chapters cited are concerned with the planned experiences with literature in the elementary classroom and with projects children can execute relating to their reading.

Whitehead, Robert. *Children's Literature: Strategies of Teaching.* Englewood Cliffs, N.J.: Prentice-Hall, Inc., 1968. Many activities with children's books are described in this publication. Many of the ideas can correlate with language experiences as children talk and write about their personal reading. Chapter 5 deals specifically with oral and written experiences with literature.

chapter seven

Prereading Skills in the Language Experience Approach

Prereading, the stage of reading development which precedes the formal introduction to reading, is the base upon which future success and attitudes toward reading are built. Readiness for reading comes from a base of past experience, maturation, and training. A successful experience in reading from the initial stages of instruction should be the goal for every beginning reader. No sharp dividing line between prereading and beginning reading should exist, but instead there should be a gradual transition from one level of reading development to the next.

Readiness for reading is multidimensional and is a composite of a number of linguistic, cognitive, physiological, perceptual, social-emotional, experiential, and other factors. However, a broad view of readiness should not obscure the need for carefully focused instruction on specific skills needed for a successful beginning reading experience. With language experience reading programs, the broad nature of overall readiness is, of course, important. The intent here is to identify selected skills and to explain language experience instruction directed toward development of those specific skills.

Language and experience are two important cornerstones on which readiness for reading is built. A language experience program can provide the foundation for a successful start in learning to read and can relate reading to the child's existing level of language development. Meaningful instruction in the skills of visual discrimination, visual memory, auditory discrimination, letter names, left-to-right progression across a line of print, and language concepts can be provided with pupil-composed materials in a language experience framework. Improving oral language facility in speaking and listening and developing an interest in reading are also concerns in the prereading period.

The language experience approach provides a natural transition from prereading to beginning reading as children are exposed to their oral language encoded in written form with personal and group experience stories. The language experience approach clearly demonstrates the relationship between spoken and written language and helps children recognize that print conveys meaning. When children first use experience stories, they may be unable to recognize any words, but gradually they do learn to identify words, thus acquiring a reading vocabulary and moving into the beginning reading stage.

The language experience approach uses functional situations with oral and written language drawn from personal experiences to develop prereading skills. This approach to prereading is not dependent upon commercial materials, although a teacher may wish to combine language experience materials with selected commercial materials. This chapter is not intended to present a complete program of instruction in prereading; rather, its intent is to describe how the language experience approach can be implemented to teach the important skills of the prereading period. While language experience is often thought of as beginning reading instead of a prereading program, there are a number of prereading applications for language experience learning.

A theme of this chapter might be "teach prereading skills in a reading situation." Print should be used in prereading to prepare children to deal with print in beginning reading. Certain readiness skills can best be developed with written language. Many commercial readiness materials contain no or very little print. By using *a reading situation* to teach prereading skills children can receive useful instruction which is applicable to the demands of beginning reading. It seems ironic that some prereading programs deprive children of the very training needed for success in beginning reading. Nonprint situations cannot provide the skill development needed in visual discrimination and left-to-right orientation which should be shown with printed words. For slow starters, especially, the prereading period may be extremely wasteful since these children may be deprived of the very experiences which would develop the reading readiness skills. Exposure to print is of prime importance in the development of readiness for reading. Another reason for recommending exposure to written language in the prereading program is that such exposure may lead to interest in learning to write, which may in turn serve as a key to motivating interest in reading.[1]

There are many avenues to reading. For example, leading children to reading by recording their speech seems to be a very natural way of leading children into reading. Using children's art work to initiate oral expression of ideas to be

[1]Dolores Durkin, "A Six Year Study of Children Who Learned to Read in School at the Age of Four," *Reading Research Quarterly* 10, No. 1 (1974–1975):11.

recorded with print is another natural way of providing a gradual transition from prereading to beginning reading.

With exposure to relevant experience materials, beginners should have an introduction to reading which presents written language in purposeful situations. However, experience materials often are used in such a general way that students may not get the specific skill training in visual discrimination, left-to-right sequence, visual memory, and language concepts essential for success in beginning reading. Attention must be focused on the appropriate cues in the print, even though the natural, relevant, and functional setting of language experience reading should not be sacrificed for skill instruction. Both the meaningful communication setting and focused skill instruction can be offered in a thorough language experience program. In the following discussion of specific skills, use of language experience materials focusing on *prereading skills in a reading situation* is recommended.

Visual Discrimination and Visual Memory

Prereading instruction should place considerable emphasis on visual discrimination and visual memory. Visual discrimination of likenesses and differences in letters and words is required in learning to read. Visual memory requires not only the ability to recognize likenesses and differences in printed language but also the ability to retain a visual image of a form. To attach a name to a printed symbol is essential to learning to read, and readers must be able to retain associations or labels for printed stimuli.

Discrimination activities with letters and words have been found to be more valuable than activities with nonword forms.[2] Distinguishing similarities and differences between letters and between words is directly related to the perceptual tasks involved in reading, whereas discriminating between pictures in a row or discriminating between geometric forms is not the same visual task as that required in reading.

Smith[3] and Samuels[4] have commented that the memory of word and letter forms seems to be related to learning distinctive features of the forms. Research confirms that when the distinctive features of letters are pointed out to prereaders, better performance in learning letter names and better discrimination have resulted than when training has not included attention to distinctive features.

Samuels[5] has presented a probing examination of research related to factors involved in success and failure in beginning reading. His examination of the

---

[2]Thomas A. Barrett, "The Relationship between Measures of Pre-reading Visual Discrimination and First Grade Reading Achievement: A Review of the Literature," *Reading Research Quarterly* 1 (Fall 1965):51.

[3]Frank Smith, *Understanding Reading* (New York: Holt, Rinehart & Winston, Inc., 1971), pp. 105–21.

[4]S. Jay Samuels, "Success and Failure in Learning to Read: A Critique of the Research," *Reading Research Quarterly* 8 (Winter 1973):213.

[5]Ibid.

research indicates that both simultaneous (matching with example shown) and successive (discrimination with example removed) training in visual discrimination should be given to facilitate learning distinctive features and to develop classification systems for memory of printed forms.

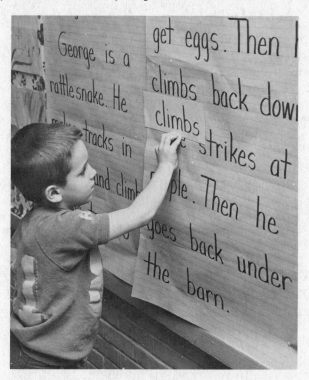

The pupil-composed materials of the language experience approach offer many opportunities for teaching both simultaneous and successive visual discrimination in a reading-type situation. For example, with the first experience stories in kindergarten and grade one, the teacher can have children match letter, word, phrase, and sentence cards to letters, words, phrases, and sentences on the charts. (See chapter 4.) This type of activity relates visual discrimination to a reading situation as children are working with meaningful content. Careful attention to the placing of the cards being matched under the appropriate corresponding material can assist in developing skill in simultaneous discrimination. While simultaneous discrimination is common, the successive type of visual discrimination is often overlooked. This type also can occur in language experience situations if after showing a particular letter, phrase, or word or sentence card, the card is removed so that children must select the appropriate response from memory. This training of memory for word forms should aid in the acquisition of a reading vocabulary.

In an activity such as writing daily plans with the class, the teacher can call the pupils' attention to the repetition of certain words. For example, plans such as the following could be written:

We will read.
We will write a story.
We will play outside.
We will have music.

The teacher can ask, "What do you notice about the first word in each line?" "What do you notice about the second word?" Word, phrase, and sentence cards can be used for matching.

In the above examples, the words have meaning for the students even though the children at the prereading level are not able to identify the words in other contexts. In the examples cited, the teacher said the word or phrase or sentence for the children to match. Pupils at the prereading level do not have to read words to respond to the task of matching visually. However, the teacher should use the word "read" in the explanations so that the children will realize that reading involves recognizing what the print represents.

Pupils' names provide another source for visual discrimination activities. A class roll chart with all the children's names can be used for matching activities. Each pupil can have an individual card with his name, and these cards can be matched to the names on the roll chart. Names with similar forms and letters can be grouped together to encourage fine discrimination. For example, names as similar as Larry and Harry, Tommy and Timmy, and Pat, Patricia, and Patrick should be grouped together.

Using pupils' names for other visual discrimination activities is also recommended. For example, a chart with horizontal rows of names can be made, and children can be directed to find all the names like the first one. The interest and motivation is usually high when pupil names are used. Names of objects in the room also can be used for teaching children to notice the first word in a line and then to identify all the other words in the line which are identical to the first one.

Letter Names

In many readiness programs, attention is given to teaching letter names. The significance of learning letter names prior to beginning reading may have been overstressed in recent years because of emphasis on the research findings that knowledge of letter names correlates more highly with reading achievement at the end of grade one than other factors.[6] The researchers' caution that correlation is not the same as cause and effect should be remembered here. Some research has found that direct instruction in letter names does not improve achievement in beginning reading.[7,8]   While prereading instruction

[6]Guy L. Bond and Robert Dykstra, "The Cooperative Research Program in First-Grade Reading Programs," *Reading Research Quarterly* 2 (Summer 1967):116.

[7]D. D. Ohnmacht, "The Effects of Letter Knowledge on Achievement in Reading in First Grade," Paper presented at American Educational Research Association, Los Angeles, California, February 1969.

[8]S. Jay Samuels, "The Effect of Letter Name Knowledge on Learning to Read," *American Educational Research Journal* 9 (Winter 1972):65–74.

should include lĕtter name knowledge as part of the program, false assumptions about the value of this instruction should be avoided.

One explanation of why a correlation exists between letter name knowledge and first grade reading achievement might be that the letter name variable is easy to identify and to test. Children who come to school knowing letter names often have a wide variety of information and the letter knowledge is just one part of the broad background they bring with them. Another point to be considered is that children who easily acquire the ability to attach a name to an abstract symbol may be more able to succeed in reading than those children who find it difficult to associate letter names and symbols. Knowing letter names is more than being able to recite the alphabet correctly. It is possible for a child to recite the alphabet and not be able to say the name of a letter when shown its printed form. Children should grasp the basic understanding that words are made up of letters and should be able to associate letter forms with letter names. Instruction in letter names is part of the "exposure" philosophy of the language experience learning in the prereading period.

In the language experience approach, letter names can be taught in functional situations since children are constantly being exposed to letters in charts, in chalkboard writing, in their names, and in personal experience stories. The name chart and experience charts suggested for visual discrimination can also be used for letter matching activities. Each child should have an individual set of all uppercase and lowercase letters to be used in the matching activities. The teacher can point to a name on the chart and ask the children to hold up the letter that they see at the beginning of that name. The name of the letter is stated by the teacher or children. In each case the name of the child should be read by the teacher so that the children realize the letter forms are used as parts of meaningful words.

The children can use their individual sets of letter cards for practice in learning letter names. Every child can respond if each has his own set of cards. For example, the teacher can say when pointing to a word on an experience chart or on the chalkboard, "This word begins with a capital *M.* Can all of you hold up your cards with capital *M?* Now can you find a little *m?*" The teacher should praise the correct responses and note those children needing additional practice.

ABC books of children's literature can be read to children to promote interest in letters. A number of the attractively illustrated and imaginatively written ABC books, such as *Bruno Munari's ABC* by Bruno Munari,[9] *ABC of Cars and Trucks* by Anne Alexander,[10] and Wanda Gag's *The ABC Bunny,*[11] should be available in the classroom library corner for pupils to examine independently. Pupils can develop their own ABC books with illustrations for each of the letters. In developing the alphabet books, letter sounds should not be stressed since confusion can result at this stage if children are confronted with the multiple associations in the sound-letter relationships of the language. In mak-

---

[9]Bruno Munari, *Bruno Munari's ABC* (New York: The World Publishing Company, 1960).
[10]Anne Alexander, *ABC of Cars and Trucks* (New York: Doubleday & Company, Inc., 1956).
[11]Wanda Gag, *The ABC Bunny* (New York: Coward-McCann, Inc., 1933).

ing class and individual ABC books the emphasis is on the names and forms of letters.

Other activities can contribute to learning letter names. Learning to write can also direct children's attention to the names and forms of letters. As letters are used in visual discrimination training, the teacher may say, "Can you find all the *l*'s in this line?" Boxes of letters may be available on the reading table, and children can be encouraged to build words to match the words in group and personal experience stories. Children can work in pairs in naming letters.

Auditory Discrimination

Learning to discriminate likenesses and differences in the sounds of spoken words has long been part of readiness programs. Prereading instruction in auditory discrimination provides a base for later instruction in phonics. While authorities differ on the importance of auditory discrimination for learning to read, a prereading program will ordinarily include auditory discrimination and auditory memory training as part of the total program.

As was true with letter name instruction, the significance of auditory discrimination in success in reading is debatable. Durrell believes that attention to distinguishing the separate sounds of spoken words is the most neglected subskill in readiness training.[12] Samuels comments, "Few areas in psychology present a more perplexing picture with conflicting viewpoints than the area of auditory discrimination."[13] Samuels comments further,

> The literature on auditory discrimination and reading leads one to conclude that in the absence of frank sensory impairment reading difficulty is probably not strongly associated with lack of auditory discrimination.
> Although auditory discrimination does not seem to be an important problem for the student learning to read, memory for letter names, sounds, or words appears to be of greater importance.[14]

Children at the beginning of grade one usually bring considerable auditory discrimination of language with them. They have learned the phonemes of their language since at the time of school entrance in first grade they can produce the phonemes of their language. Probably what teachers mean when they say that children need training in auditory discrimination is that children need to learn the terminology such as "sound," "beginning sound," "ending sound," "rhyme," and where they need to focus their attention for learning sound-symbol correspondences.

Some children do poorly on auditory discrimination tests partly because of lack of comprehension of the directions, partly because the words used are in

---

[12]Donald D. Durrell, "Learning Factors in Beginning Reading," in *Teaching Young Children to Read*, ed. Warren G. Cutts (Washington, D.C.: U.S. Office of Education, 1964), p. 72.

[13]Samuels, "Success and Failure," p. 226.

[14]Ibid, pp. 232–33.

isolation and may not be pronounced by the examiner as they are in the child's speech, and partly because of lack of familiarity with the task required rather than lack of the ability to discriminate.

In initial reading instruction attention is given to the *association* of a sound with the printed letter symbol. Prior to that type of instruction, the ability to discriminate similarities and differences in sounds in spoken words is particularly important.

Numerous opportunities for auditory discrimination grow out of language experience activities. As group experience charts are written with pupils, attention can be directed to words on a chart which begin with the same sound. For example, with the chart on p. 32, the teacher might say, "Listen as I say these words: carrots, cabbage; go, get. Listen for the first sound in them."

The name chart described on p. 82 can also be used for auditory discrimination as the teacher can ask pupils to listen for similarities in the beginning sounds of several names such as Jack, Johnny, Joyce. Groups of three names, two of which have the same beginning sound and one with a different beginning sound can be used as children are asked to indicate which two names begin alike.

In personal experience stories, teachers can point out to a child that two or more words begin with the same sound and have him say the words to hear the sound. Work on rhyming words should also be included when examples of these words appear in the group and individual experience stories.

Some children who may seem confused about auditory discrimination activities with words may need some experiences to develop the concept of "sound" and "alike and different." For children who seem unable to distinguish between letter sounds in spoken words, more gross auditory discrimination may be advisable. To develop an awareness of sounds in the environment before progressing to letter sounds, children's literature books such as *The Listening Walk* by Paul Showers[15] and the series of "Noisy Books" by Margaret Wise Brown[16] can be very helpful.

Left-to-Right Direction

Following a line of print from left-to-right is a requirement of the reading act. This skill must be taught carefully, and the correct orientation to the printed page must be established in the prereading period. Developing the habit of observing printed words and sentences from left-to-right should be a major focus of the skill training of the prereading period.

Language experience materials can be used to demonstrate left-to-right sequence in reading situations. In other words, left-to-right is taught not by observing rows of pictures but with printed letters and words, thereby relating

---

[15]Paul Showers, *The Listening Walk* (New York: Crowell Collier & Macmillan, Inc., 1961).

[16]For example, see Margaret Wise Brown, *The City Noisy Book* (New York: Harper & Row, Publishers, 1939).

the training to the task needed in reading. The major advantage of the language experience approach activities for teaching left-to-right progression is the natural relationship of this skill to the actual reading situations.

As the teacher writes and reads plans, she can show left-to-right direction by telling pupils that in writing one always starts at the left side and goes to the right. As the teacher reads she should move her hand from left-to-right under the words. In the reading of all group experience stories, the left-to-right direction can be demonstrated by the teacher's hand movement or a pointer. As pupils match cards to a chart, the teacher can show left-to-right direction. In working with personal experience stories, the teacher can show individual pupils how to read print from left-to-right. As pupils underline words on the board, on a chart, or in a personal experience story, the teacher again can encourage left-to-right progression. As pupils learn to do manuscript writing, left-to-right direction also should be taught. Of course, game-type activities with left and right directions such as "Simon Says" and "Looby Loo" can be used.

Oral Language

Increasing oral language facility is another concern in the prereading program since the ability to comprehend and express ideas through oral language contributes to meaningful reading. Both receptive and productive language situations are important. There must be something to talk about, but, while starting with pupil backgrounds, the teacher must not limit the exposure of pupils to only that language and those experiences which they presently possess. It is the teacher's obligation to extend the experience background and to promote further language competence and performance. In the language experience approach with the integration of speaking, listening, reading, and writing, oral language experiences receive considerable attention.

Children must be *encouraged* to talk in situations where they feel free to express themselves regardless of their level of language development and of their language patterns. Children must be *encouraged* to talk when stimuli for conversation and discussion are ample and ever-changing. Children must be *encouraged* to talk where pupil talk is regarded as more important than teacher talk. Children must be *encouraged* to talk in situations where they are exposed to new experiences, new vocabulary, and new thoughts through tapes, stories, trips, films, and pictures. Children must be *encouraged* to talk in an environment where their talk is the basis for other language experiences as they compose group and personal experience stories and class and individual books, as they listen to the ideas of others and state their own, and as they read their ideas.

Language Concepts

Developing children's concepts of language should be included in prereading and beginning reading instruction. Language experience materials are particularly valuable in developing children's understanding of language concepts. In the matching activities suggested for visual discrimination, the concepts of word, phrase, letter, and sentence can be demonstrated functionally. The orientation to written language offered with language experience stories can provide a base for developing the concepts of language often lacking in the prereading and beginning reading stages.

It is well known that most children who enter kindergarten and first grade bring with them considerable language mastery. While this mastery is far from complete, the level of linguistic development does include ability to use the basic sentence patterns of the native language, knowledge of the meaning of thousands of words, and the ability to communicate both as a language receiver and language producer. While the linguistic performance and competence is extensive, it seems parodoxical to note that children are often confused by the terminology used in beginning reading. (See p. 59.)

Interest in Reading

Before formal instruction in reading is begun, it is important that children develop a desire to read. Children who have been read to at home or in nursery school and kindergarten have experienced pleasurable contacts with books. For those children who have not had such contacts, providing opportunities to hear stories and to examine the attractive picture-story books is even more important. The most effective means for developing an interest in reading is through exposure to interesting children's literature materials. Realizing that meaning comes from the printed page and that reading is an enjoyable experience are understandings conveyed through hearing stories read aloud. Every classroom should contain an attractive library corner, and every classroom should feature a daily period of story reading by the teacher.

The personal pride that results from pupil authorship also has a favorable effect on pupil interest. The group and individual experience stories written with children in the prereading and beginning reading stages should foster enthusiasm for reading since the content is of high interest to pupils. If the introduction to reading occurs in a functional situation, interest should be inherent in that situation. Success with the pupil-composed materials should also have a favorable effect on attitude and interest.

Summary

One of the most significant contributions of language experience instruction to the prereading stage is the development of the general understanding that print represents meaning. Prereading instruction in visual discrimination and visual memory, letter names, auditory discrimination, left-to-right progression, language development, language concepts, and interest in reading can be approached from a language experience framework. Particular emphasis is placed on encouraging oral language development since this is the base from which other language experiences grow. Children's oral language forms the basis of pupil-produced materials which can be used for skill instruction in prereading.

In the language experience approach, the prereading stage blends gradually into the beginning reading stage through the use of group experience charts and personal experience stories. The language experience approach to prereading illustrates the relationship between spoken and written language. Prereading training in the language experience approach develops skills needed for beginning reading in a reading situation with functional, pupil-developed materials rather than with artificial materials remote from children's experiences. Prereading and beginning reading are introduced in a situation which fosters success and healthy attitudes toward self and toward learning.

Suggested Readings

Durkin, Dolores. *Teaching Young Children to Read.* Boston: Allyn and Bacon, 1972. Durkin presents a thorough consideration of the topic of readiness and gives detailed descriptions for instruction in prereading and beginning reading.

Lee, Dorris M., and Van Allen, R. *Learning to Read through Experience.* New York: Appleton-Century-Crofts, 1963. This basic source on the language experience approach gives many examples of the transition from prereading to initial reading instruction. The philosophy of the language experience approach as a natural introduction to reading is a basic theme of this book.

Samuels, S. Jay. "Success and Failure in Learning to Read: A Critique of the Research," *Reading Research Quarterly* 8 (Winter 1973): 200–39. For a thoughtful analysis of research related to learning to read in the beginning stages, this source is recommended.

Wilson, Robert M., and Hall, MaryAnne, *Reading and the Elementary School Child.* New York: Van Nostrand Reinhold, 1972, Chapter 5. A discussion of factors important in readiness for reading and suggestions for instruction are included.

chapter eight

Teaching Reading Skills in the Language Experience Approach

The theory and techniques of the preceding chapters have been concerned with teaching children to read effectively. Because the language experience approach is so concerned with reading as communication through language symbols, the place of skill instruction may be unclear for several reasons. First, since in the language experience approach reading is viewed as a *process* rather than as a collection of skills, skills do not determine the instructional content. Second, since the language experience approach is built from pupils' oral language, the dimension of skill instruction may not be clearly recognized. Third, since the language experience approach is an integrated one, with the language skills taught *through* pupil composition and experiences with spoken and written language, a teacher may not be clear about the types and amounts of direct skill instruction which should be offered. Fourth, the language experience approach is not one with a clear, systematic sequence of learning according to a predetermined guide. The purpose of this chapter is to identify selected reading skills and to suggest means of incorporating skill instruction in the language experience framework by discussing word attack, comprehension, and oral reading. In skill instruction, as in other language experience learning, attention must be on language as communication—not on small portions of that language which are devoid of meaning without context.

Word Attack Skills in the
Language Experience Approach

Word attack skills are accorded immense attention in the teaching of reading. In fact, in some reading programs the emphasis on word attack seems disproportionate when considered in connection with attention to meaningful reading. Focus on word attack, word recognition, and phoneme-grapheme correspondences may put too much stress on the word and letter units of language instead of on larger units of meaning. Teaching children to recognize and respond to printed language is broader than the teaching of what is traditionally referred to as word attack. Perhaps the use of the term *language recognition* might be more appropriate than the terms *word attack* or *word recognition.* Effective teaching strategies in language experience reading rest upon having children develop language recognition skills. Language recognition skills include the strategies children need to deal with graphophonic, semantic, and syntactic language information. In fact, much of the material in previous chapters is more related to language recognition than the material included here with the word attack label.

Any reading program must teach children methods of attacking unfamiliar words quickly and independently. Each teacher must be knowledgeable about the content of word attack, provide both direct and incidental instruction, and evaluate children's learning in this area. In order to strengthen the reading program while following a language experience plan of reading instruction, some authorities recommend that the teacher follow a systematic, definite program in word attack skills in addition to the other language experience activities.

Flexible grouping for skill instruction in the language experience approach is recommended since groups will be formed on the basis of need for a common skill and will either be disbanded or modified in composition as needs change. Teachers can follow checklists of skills in phonics and structural analysis and keep a record for each child in order to note when a skill has been mastered and to indicate those skills which need to be learned. Many teachers keep a notebook or file box of informal observations about each child's reading performance.

The language experience approach does offer an excellent means for reinforcing skill training in functional situations. The language experience approach can teach skills as needed by pupils in their independent reading and writing. Pupils' language in the group and individual stories and in their word banks will provide examples to be used in the skill instruction. The skills usually thought to be necessary for independence in word attack are configuration, phonics, structural analysis, context clues, and use of the dictionary.

In chart 1, the reader will find an overview of the content of phonics and structural analysis in a form which can be used for recording a child's progress. Prereading skills in letter name knowledge, visual discrimination, and auditory discrimination are included. Space is provided for recording when a skill is taught and when it is mastered. The checklist is written with descriptions of the child's behavior which would demonstrate skill competency. For more complete discussions of word attack content, see the suggested readings at the end of the chapter.

CHART 1

Word Attack Checklist

Child_____

Prereading

Can auditorily discriminate between likenesses and differences in beginning sounds

Taught   Mastered

_____   _____

Can auditorily discriminate by recognizing rhyming words

Taught   Mastered

_____   _____

Can identify letter forms by name

Taught   Mastered

_____   _____

Can visually discriminate by matching capital letter forms*

Taught   Mastered

_____   _____

Can visually discriminate by matching lowercase letter forms*

Taught   Mastered

_____   _____

Can visually discriminate by matching word forms*

Taught   Mastered

_____   _____

Consonants

Single Consonants: b, hard c, soft c, d, f, hard g, soft g, h, j, k, l, m, n, p, qu, r, s, t, v, w, x, y, z
_____

*Both simultaneous and successive discrimination should be included (see p. 81).

Can identify in initial position in words

Taught   Mastered

_____   _____

Can identify in medial position in words

Taught   Mastered

_____   _____

Can identify in final position in words

Taught   Mastered

_____   _____

Can substitute consonants to attack new words

in initial position (Jack to back)

Taught   Mastered

_____   _____

in final position (bed to beg)

Taught   Mastered

_____   _____

Consonant blends or clusters: *l* blends: bl, cl, fl, gl, pl, sl, spl
r blends: br, cr, dr, fr, gr, pr, tr, scr, spr, str, thr
s blends: sc, sk, sl, sm, sn, sp, st, sw, str

Can identify *l* blends in spoken and written words

Taught   Mastered

_____   _____

Can identify *r* blends in spoken and written words

Taught   Mastered

_____   _____

Can identify *s* blends in spoken and written words

Taught   Mastered

_____   _____

Can substitute blends to attack new words

Taught   Mastered

_____   _____

Consonant Digraphs: sh, ch, wh, th (both voiced and unvoiced)

Can identify in spoken and written words

Taught   Mastered

_____   _____

Can substitute digraphs to attack new words

Taught   Mastered

_____   _____

Vowels

Long, short, r-controlled sounds

Can recognize long vowel sounds in spoken and written words

Taught   Mastered

_____   _____

Can recognize short vowel sounds in spoken and written words

Taught   Mastered

_____   _____

Can recognize *r*-controlled vowel sounds in spoken and written words

Taught   Mastered

_____   _____

Other vowel sounds: long oo, short oo, oi and oy diphthong, ou and ow diph-thong, y as long i and long e.

Can recognize long and short *oo* in spoken and written words

Taught   Mastered

_____   _____

Can recognize *oi* and *oy* diphthong in spoken and written words

Taught   Mastered

_____   _____

Can recognize *y* as long i and long e in spoken and written words

Taught   Mastered

_____   _____

Vowel generalizations: The generalizations which apply to these key words (1) gō, (2) gĕt, (3) rāin, (4) rīde

Can state and apply generalization No. 1

Taught   Mastered

_____   _____

Can state and apply generalization No. 2

Taught   Mastered

_____   _____

Can state and apply generalization No. 3.

Taught   Mastered

_____   _____

Can state and apply generalization No. 4.

Taught   Mastered

_____   _____

Syllabication*

Generalizations: 1. vccv   2. vcv   3. c + le = last syllable
                       lad/der   lā/dy   lā/dle

Can state and apply generalization No. 1.

Taught   Mastered

_____   _____

Can state and apply generalization No. 2.

Taught   Mastered

_____   _____

Can state and apply generalization No. 3.

Taught   Mastered

_____   _____

Can apply vowel generalizations to determine vowel sounds in syllables.

Taught   Mastered

_____   _____

Structural Analysis

Compound words, contractions, roots, prefixes, and suffixes

Can recognize and attack compound words

Taught   Mastered

_____   _____

Can recognize and attack contractions

Taught   Mastered

_____   _____

Can recognize and attack words with roots, prefixes, and suffixes
Taught   Mastered

_____   _____

Structural Changes: (1) Drop silent *e* (ride to riding) (2) double consonant (hop
                         to hopping) (3) *y* to *i* (candy to candies)

_____

*The value of teaching syllabication is questionable according to some authorities (see Suggested Readings).

Can read and spell words following generalization No. 1.

Taught	Mastered
_____	_____

Can read and spell words following generalization No. 2.

Taught	Mastered
_____	_____

Can read and spell words following generalization No. 3.

Taught	Mastered
_____	_____

Another kind of record which can be useful for teachers would be similar to chart 2. This record can be kept as certain skills are stressed with a notation of which skills have been taught to and mastered by individuals.

CHART 2

STUDENT	INITIAL CONSONANTS																					
	b	c	d	f	g	h	j	k	l	m	n	p	qu	r	s	t	v	w	y	z
Ann	x	x	x	x	x	x	x	x	x	x	x	x	x	x	x	x	x	x	x	x
Sue	x	x	x	x	x	x	x	x	x	x	x	x	x	x	x	x	x	x	x	x
Bob	x	x	x	x	x	x														
Kathy	x	x	/	/	/	/														
David	/	/	/	/	/	/														

/ = *taught*   x = *mastered*

At a glance, it is possible to tell which skills have been introduced to and mastered by individuals. For example, as recorded on chart 2, Ann and Sue have mastered all of the phoneme-grapheme relationships for consonants in the initial position in words. By studying the same chart, one finds that David has not mastered the content to which he has been exposed. Such records can be helpful as a record of instruction and for noting progress, as a basis for forming skill groups, and as a source of information for conferences with parents.

CONFIGURATION

Configuration clues about the general shape or form of a word are some of the first techniques used in reading as children learn to recognize words. When children begin to read experience stories and add words to the word banks, they are using configuration clues as they acquire a reading vocabulary. For specific instruction in configuration, the teacher may provide practice during group experience story activities. Pupils match word cards to cards on the chart, find words that begin a particular way, and circle or frame certain words. The procedures are really an extension of visual discrimination begun in the pre-reading period. Developing children's memory for word forms is an aim of initial reading instruction, and configuration practice should be done in such a way as to foster instead of detract from memory of word forms.

For individual work with configuration, the personal experiences stories and word banks offer excellent materials for practice. A child can match words in the word bank to the words in his stories, he can underline known words, he can find words with similar configuration such as *can* and *car,* and *look* and *book,* and he can compare likenesses and differences in words. The goal of such configuration practice and exposure to word forms is to add to the reading vocabulary, the stock of words recognized instantly when seen in print. Any good reader must have a large reading vocabulary, and the teacher must seek to constantly enlarge children's reading vocabularies through many language experience activities.

PHONICS

In working with phonics in the language experience approach, an analytic approach which refers to studying speech sounds in whole words rather than studying single sounds in isolation is preferred. In an analytic approach, known words are used in developing an understanding of the phoneme-grapheme (sound-letter) relationships of the language.

In the teaching of the association of a sound with its printed counterpart, the teacher must provide auditory and visual experience with the sound and letter form and must demonstrate the application of the phoneme-grapheme relationship to attack an unfamiliar word in context. Since phonics instruction aims to equip children with a tool for attacking unfamiliar words, the application step must be stressed. For example, in working with the initial sound of "m," the teacher may group several children together and ask them to find all of the words in their word banks which begin with "m." The instruction should include hearing the sound of "m" as the words are said aloud. Then, several words familiar to all the pupils should be listed so that children can see the visual form of "m" in whole word forms. Then some sentences can be written with a new word beginning with "m" in each sentence. The children can attack these words by using the phonic and context clues. Examples might be, "When it is cold, you wear *mittens,*" or "The *milk* is white." The children can be told that they know all the words except the one beginning with "m" and are told to think of a word which would make sense in each sentence.

Words which are already known by children can be used to illustrate the consonant substitution technique for attacking new words. The teacher might say, "You know the word ten. What word do you have if the *t* is changed to an *m*?" Additional examples such as *bat* to *mat, six* to *mix* could be used.

A similar procedure can be followed in teaching the sound-letter relationships of the other consonants, the consonant blends or clusters, the consonant digraphs, and the vowel sounds.

STRUCTURAL ANALYSIS

Structural analysis involves attacking unfamiliar words by analyzing word parts or morphemic units. A morpheme is the smallest unit of meaning in the language. In structural analysis children must be taught to look for compound words, roots, prefixes, suffixes, contractions, and known syllables. The last part of the word-attack checklist (chart 1) lists the major categories of structural analysis. Flexible grouping of pupils for direct instruction is recommended while working with the checklist content.

These skills can be taught through examples from the personal and group experience stories and the word banks. Structural analysis of prefixes and suffixes should be illustrated in sentence context. In working with prefixes and suffixes, emphasis must be on meaning, not just on form or pronunciation. It is more valuable for a child to use meaningful sentences to decide whether *wish*, *wishes, wished*, or *wishing* is appropriate than merely to drill on or write the word *wish* with endings, since it is only in a sentence context that a child will know which form is appropriate.

Botel describes a discovery procedure for developing the understanding of generalizations. Children are given auditory and visual examples with a particular pattern. They are then directed to observe the pattern through careful teacher questioning, to collect words which follow the pattern, and to formulate the appropriate generalization for the pattern.[1]

For example, if children were working with the structural change generalization in which the final consonant is doubled in a word having a consonant-vowel-consonant (*hop*) pattern before adding an ending, the discovery procedure would work as follows: The teacher could write several pairs of sentences such as, "Jack will bat next," "He has a good batting average," or "The car will stop at the light," "The car has stopped." She could then ask, "Can you find the root word in *batting?*" "Does the ending begin with a vowel or a consonant?" "What is added to the root word before adding the ending?" "Look at the last three letters of the root words." Children should note the consonant-vowel-consonant pattern of the root words. They can be asked to find words in their reading which fit this pattern. In the inductive learning of the discovery procedure, the generalization is stated by the children after specific examples are studied.

The preceding procedure can be used regardless of the instructional approach in reading. However, in the language experience approach, the distinctive characteristic is the selection of words from the children's writing. The above procedure can be applied to the examples listed in chart 1 for vowel generalizations, syllabication generalizations, and structural analysis.

---

[1]Morton Botel, *How to Teach Reading*, 4th Ed. (Chicago: Follett Publishing Company, 1968), pp. 64–65.

CONTEXT

Context clues in word attack refer to the use of surrounding reading material to determine the meaning and pronunciation of an unfamiliar word. Effective use of context is dependent upon the syntactical patterns of language to derive meaning from print. Isolated word study deprives the reader of syntactical and semantic clues found in larger units of language. Because the language experience approach works with meaningful materials in sentence and story contexts, the use of context clues can be easily taught and applied. As children first learn to read their spoken language, the use of context reading is evident. When a child does not know a word while reading a sentence, the teacher may say, "If you remember the rest of what you read you may be able to figure out the word."

Contextual closure exercises which omit one word from a sentence can be developed with material from language experience stories. For example, a teacher may take sentences from a group experience story, write them on the board, on a transparency for the overhead projector, or on another chart. She can then ask the children if they can select from the words written on word cards or on the board the word which belongs in a particular sentence. Closure activities can be done in the same manner with individual stories with words from word banks. Small groups can be formed with children reading sentences from their individual stories, leaving out a word, and asking the group members to suggest the appropriate word. Such activity helps to teach the concept of synonyms and can extend both the speaking and reading vocabularies. The use of context clues is also combined with phonic and structural clues in attacking unfamiliar words.

DICTIONARY

Functional and informal dictionary activities can be included in the language experience framework. The interest in word study, which was a theme of chapter 5, should encourage children to be enthusiastic about using dictionaries. As children read and write independently, they should be encouraged to use the dictionary as an aid to meaning, spelling, and pronunciation. At every grade level in the elementary school, dictionaries should always be available for reference in the classroom writing center and reading corner. A number of easy, attractively-illustrated picture dictionaries are now available for beginning readers. Beyond the primary levels, other commercial dictionaries can be provided.

All of the word bank experiences with alphabetizing and word meaning should facilitate dictionary study. Word banks can lead to the development of class and individual dictionaries as children compile definitions and alphabetize and list words in dictionary form in a notebook. The concept of multiple meanings can be developed through discussion of the words in word banks, and children can compose a group bank of "Words with More than One Meaning."

Alphabetizing in functional situations with language experience activities can be included in the total program. For example, in one primary class the children made a class dictionary of names, addresses, and telephone numbers. The original purpose was to have a list for sending Christmas and Valentine cards. The teacher explained that directories are alphabetized according to the last name. The games and activities listed in the pamphlet *Fun with Words*[2] and the activities suggested at the beginning of the *Junior* and *Beginning Thorndike-Barnhart Dictionaries* (Scott, Foresman and Co.) can make the teaching of dictionary skills lively and interesting.

Comprehension in the Language Experience Approach

Instruction in reading must promote thinking as children react to written language. Without comprehension, reading is of little value. Comprehension in reading can be viewed as the process of reconstructing a message from print or as the processing of information presented through print. Language experience reading is especially advantageous in showing the process of reading as one of reconstructing meaning from print. The importance of comprehension in reading is shown through all language experience activities, and one of the major advantages of this approach is the use of material with high meaning. Developing comprehension strategies must be done with meaningful language, and developing comprehension does not come from isolated word and letter study, which is usually a nonreading and a noncommunication situation.

Reading programs give considerable attention to "comprehension skills." Lists of skills can be found in most methods textbooks as well as the basal reading series and curriculum guides. A skill explanation of comprehension may help make instruction better focused than instruction without a skill emphasis. However, a skill explanation alone may not give sufficient attention to the process of interpretation and to the levels of thinking required in reading.

Reading is often described as a thinking process. Taxonomies such as Bloom's levels of thinking[3] and Barrett's four level taxonomy (literal, inference, evaluation, and appreciation) for reading[4] are useful in helping teachers become aware of the type of thinking required in reading. In teaching reading as a thinking process, teachers need to require children to read beyond the literal level. Children should search for deeper meanings as they interpret an author's words in light of personal experiences and as they seek answers to questions which involve more than recalling facts. Careful questioning by the teacher on various levels of comprehension is essential. The detailed descriptions of questions by Sanders in *Classroom Questions*[5] is particularly helpful. Teachers will

[2] *Fun with Words* (Glenview, Ill.: Scott, Foresman and Company, 1962).

[3] Benjamin S. Bloom, *Taxonomy of Educational Objectives: Handbook, Cognitive Domain* (New York: David McKay Co., 1956).

[4] Richard J. Smith and Thomas Barrett, *Teaching Reading in the Middle Grades* (Reading, Mass.: Addison-Wesley, 1974).

[5] Norris M. Sanders, *Classroom Questions* (New York: Harper and Row, Publishers, 1966).

find extensive discussions of teaching comprehension included in a number of textbooks on reading methodology (see Suggested Readings). In the language experience approach there is probably less questioning about what is read than with other approaches. However, some questioning can be conducted in connection with language experience reading, but the creativity and interest in language experience activities should not be sacrificed to provide skill instruction.

Not all comprehension tasks can be taught through pupil-composed materials. While children can understand the meaning of their own stories, care must be exercised to ensure that children are equipped to derive meaning from materials written by others. Exposure to many types of materials is essential, especially beyond the initial stages of reading. Children should be given extensive opportunities to read the stories of other children and to react through discussion in group situations to the meaning of various materials.

For children who have been diagnosed as having difficulty in comprehension, the language experience approach may be a very helpful remediation procedure. Some remedial students as well as children in the early stages of reading instruction seem unaware that print represents meaning. If children regard reading as a process of naming words, comprehension will suffer. Language experience teaching is one method for demonstrating that written language represents meaningful ideas.

After beginners and remedial students realize that their ideas can be represented in writing, these students need instruction focusing on understanding ideas in materials in addition to the language experience creations.

All of the comments stated throughout this book on the importance of communication in the reading process and in the language experience framework of learning and teaching are relevant to teaching comprehension in reading. Attention to increasing vocabulary and to facilitating expression in spoken and written language contribute to the interpretation of reading material. Exposure to literature read orally also requires interpretation of language symbols and enriches the knowledge background. As children react to one another's writing positively and constructively, they are actively involved in obtaining meaning from print.

Oral Reading in the Language Experience Approach

Helping children communicate through expressive oral reading is another concern of the teacher of elementary reading skills. Oral reading in the elementary school should occur in functional situations and should not be done in a mechanical or routine manner.

The language experience approach has distinct advantages for teaching oral reading. This approach, which uses children's spoken language, presents an excellent means for helping children realize that in reading they must supply the intonation of spoken language. Instead of working with unnatural word-by-word recitation of controlled vocabulary materials, the teacher can teach oral reading from the beginning stages as a way of making print sound like the spoken language. Sentence patterns which are already in a child's speech form the basis for reading words in meaningful sentence patterns with the characteristic juncture, pitch, and stress normally employed in speech. For disadvantaged children, the use of their own experience stories is particularly important since reading textbooks do not use their sentence patterns, making the task of reading especially difficult. From the time of the recording of the first group and individual experience stories, the teacher should demonstrate fluent oral reading when reading the stories to the children. Although some teachers tend to read in such a way as to distort the speech patterns with their desire to have children observe individual words carefully, word-by-word emphasis is to be avoided. Children should employ expressive reading naturally as they read print which was originally an oral story.

Gradually discussion of punctuation clues for intonation will occur through the individual and group pupil-composed materials. The function of punctuation is shown as the teacher points out, "This is the end of your thought, so we'll put a period or a dot. The next line is a new sentence, so it will begin with a capital letter." Instruction of this nature should not overshadow the writing and reading experience but can be included occasionally.

Oral reading should be taught since it requires some skills in oral communication in addition to the other reading skills. The teaching of oral reading requires more than merely saying the content of instructional reading materials aloud.

Meaningful oral reading can be provided easily with language experience instruction since children are usually eager to share their creative efforts with others. Audience type situations, such as reading the individual and class books to other classes, can demonstrate to children the importance of effective oral reading. Small, flexible groups can be formed within classes for sharing stories. As children read their own and their classmates' stories, they can practice effective oral reading. Children can tape their stories, and the tapes can be replayed for personal evaluation of the oral reading.

Silent reading should receive greater emphasis than oral reading since too much emphasis on the latter can be detrimental to the development of a satisfactory rate of silent reading. Since oral reading without meaning is a barrier to comprehension and since the majority of reading tasks require silent reading, such emphasis is essential. In the language experience activities as well as in experiences with other reading materials, children should first read silently that which they are asked to read aloud.

Oral reading serves as a diagnostic tool for the teacher as she notes indications of difficulty and analyzes patterns of errors or particular weaknesses.

Summary

Effective teaching of reading must include the teaching of strategies for written language recognition. In instructional programs, attention should be given to word attack, comprehension, and oral reading. While the creative, communicative, personal, and functional attributes of the language experience approach are so important, acquisition of reading skills should not be neglected. Many functional situations in the language experience approach may be utilized to illustrate or to reinforce particular skills. It is recommended that the teacher offer both direct and indirect skill instruction in the areas discussed in this chapter.

Suggested Readings

Botel, Morton. *How to Teach Reading,* 4th Ed. Chicago: Follett Publishing Company, 1968. Step-by-step teaching procedures are outlined with specific examples. A brief overview of the content of word attack is given, and the use of questions for developing comprehension is explained clearly.

Groff, Patrick. "Fifteen Flaws of Phonics," *Elementary English* 50 (January 1972): 35–40. Groff's article requires that a teacher reexamine beliefs about the teaching of phonics.

Heilman, Arthur. *Phonics in Proper Perspective,* 3d Ed. Columbus: Charles E. Merrill Publishing Company, 1976. This paperback book contains an overview of phonics content in reading as well as clear procedures for teaching word attack skills.

Sanders, Norris M. *Classroom Questions.* New York: Harper and Row, Publishers, 1966. A classification of types of questions is clearly elaborated. Using questions of the types discussed in this source can promote depth in reading comprehension.

Smith, Frank. *Understanding Reading.* New York: Holt, Rinehart and Winston, 1971. This probing psycholinguistic analysis of the reading process raises many questions about how reading is learned and about which language cues are helpful to a reader.

Wilson, Robert M., and Hall, MaryAnne. *Programmed Word Attack for Teachers,* 2d Ed. Columbus: Charles E. Merrill Publishing Company, 1974. For the teacher unfamiliar with the content of word attack, this programmed text provides a comprehensive overview.

Zuck, L. V. "Some Questions about the Teaching of Syllabication Rules," *The Reading Teacher* 27 (March 1974): 583–88. Zuck presents the argument that teaching of syllabication is not useful.

chapter nine

The Language Experience Classroom

Reading as a language experience has been described, and the instructional dimensions have been explored in the preceding chapters. Now, in summary, certain overall concerns of the teacher who wishes to employ this approach are examined in this chapter. What is the classroom environment like? How is the language experience classroom organized? How is learning evaluated in the language experience approach?

The Language Experience Teacher

The most important single influence on learning in any given classroom is the teacher. Attitudes, rapport with children, arrangement of stimuli for learning, and knowledge and skill are hard to measure objectively but are extremely influential in the teacher's effectiveness.

Teachers' expectations of children's performance affect learning. Language experience teachers must believe that children can learn through personal involvement in situations requiring communication and that children's ability to use language effectively can be developed through the use of *their* language as the base of teaching and learning.

The teacher's interpretation of reading and of the processes of learning and teaching in relation to the individual influences the effectiveness of her teaching. In the language experience approach, the teacher *must* encourage freedom of expression in a setting in which creativity can flourish in order to promote growth in the ability to communicate.

Essential attitudes of the teacher in the language experience framework of teaching reading are:

1. The teacher must accept each child's language *as it is*, not as the teacher wishes it to be.
2. The teacher must recognize the creative nature of the language experience approach.
3. The teacher must recognize reading as a language activity which serves as a communication tool and must then integrate the teaching of reading and language.

In all language activities the teacher must accept the child's language as it is; the teacher must not convey rejection by altering the language in order to have grammatically correct sentences which are not the actual recording of a child's speech. Allen states, " . . . , it is important to remember that each child has a natural language and that new language learnings must be related to it, faulty as it may be."[1] In their concern for developing language facility, teachers must be careful not to reject a child's existing level of communication skills. Facility in language skills will be fostered by opportunities for communicating personally valued ideas, not by a program of intensive correction. In the early stages, correction of speech may serve to block oral and written expression rather than to encourage it. Lefevre warns:

> If teachers insist on instant correction, incessant correction, of every so-called mistake the child makes in speech, reading, and writing, the child will close up like an oyster. He will hate to recite and hate to write in school.[2]

Every child makes many mistakes in learning to talk, but with opportunity and experience he develops the ability to communicate through speech. The process of communication is more important than the correctness of the mechanics. The preceding statements should not imply that children be encouraged to learn incorrect speech patterns; instead these statements emphasize that the first concern in the early stages of instruction is to develop the understanding that thoughts can be communicated orally and encoded with written symbols which then can be read with understanding. The teacher does have a responsibility to provide appropriate language models and to provide opportunities for expression so that communication skill does improve.

[1] R. Van Allen, *Attitudes and the Art of Teaching Reading* (Washington, D.C.: National Educational Association, 1965), p. 6.

[2] Carl A. Lefevre, "Language and Self: Fulfillment of Trauma? Part I," *Elementary English* 43 (February 1966):127.

Acceptance is a key word for the teacher who recognizes the creative nature of the language experience approach. An attitude and climate of acceptance must be present if creativity is to flourish. Wilt comments on the importance of accepting a child's creative effort:

> The teacher should accept enthusiastically and generously whatever personal expression the child dreams up. Regardless of the creative result, he must always realize that the process is of far more consequence than the product.[3]

The language experience teacher will need to believe sincerely that children can be creative if teachers permit that creativity to be expressed and if they seek to reach it in a variety of ways. Teachers must believe in and develop pupil authorship.

Much has been stated in the preceding material concerning the stress on the interrelatedness of language and reading in the language experience approach. Acknowledgment of this concept is so important, however, that this third basic attitude of the teacher of recognition that reading and language should be taught as an integrated process is stressed again. The teacher has the responsibility for presenting situations which stimulate ever-increasing facility with language. The chasm which has often existed in elementary schools between the teaching of language and the teaching of reading is bridged in the language experience approach. Reading is viewed, not as a separate subject, but as a part of the language program. As children learn to communicate more effectively orally, they are learning to communicate more effectively through reading.

Classroom Organization in the Language Experience Approach

In facilitating instruction in the language experience approach, whole group, small group, and individual learning situations are utilized. While individualization of instruction is a prime consideration, group instruction is desirable for certain experiences and, in many cases, is more efficient than individual instruction. However, the individual nature of the language experience approach is one of its major attributes and individual response of a personal and unique nature is to be encouraged constantly. Large group experiences can often lead to different individual activities for each child as he creates his personal reading materials.

Literature experiences, group experience stories, planning sessions, and creative writing can occur with a total class group. Group interaction through discussion is valuable since in this way children learn to be careful listeners, to respect and respond to the ideas of others, and to express their ideas in ways

---

[3]Miriam E. Wilt, *Creativity in the Elementary School* (New York: Appleton-Century-Crofts, 1959), p. 8.

to be understood by others. Certain language activities involving word banks can also be used with large groups.

Small group instruction is desirable for the sharing of personal writing, for instruction in skills, and for directed instruction in reading for those pupils with the same reading level or those who are working on the same specific skill. Small groups can be temporary and can be disbanded when no longer needed. Pupils can work together in small groups without teacher direction as they share writing, talk about words, and discuss their independent reading.

Children can work in pairs or in teams. These pairs or teams can read orally to each other, can work together in building sentences with the word banks, and can share their individual stories. Small groups can be formed on an interest basis as children who have written or have read materials on a particular topic share their information. Projects on which several children work together provide another situation for small group instruction.

Individual instruction is offered when a teacher records a child's personal story and when selected rereading activities are conducted with the story. (See p. 34.) Using the individualized reading approach in conjunction with the language experience approach is favored by many teachers. The individual pupil-teacher conference is utilized in both the individualized and language experience approaches to instruction. In the conference situation the teacher observes a child's reading needs, suggests material for future reading, and provides needed skill instruction.

When organizing a language experience instructional program, the teacher should look at the total language program, not just at the reading program. The language experience activities described in this book rest upon a philosophy of integration of all the language arts.

The language experience classroom should provide ideas and materials for worthwhile independent activities in the language arts. Teachers are concerned about the time needed for language experience instruction. Classroom organization which uses language experience activities for independent learning adds considerably to the effectiveness of the approach and to the efficient use of time since much learning can occur in the self-directed activities. Learning centers which offer planned reinforcement of specific learning and through which children can pursue individual interests are featured in increasing numbers in today's classrooms. Additional experiences with a particular skill or topic can be done independently in the learning centers. Learning centers offer activities which are not required or standardized for all children but which serve as an opportunity for encouraging and extending pupil interests. Learning centers of particular importance in the implementation of the language experience approach are a reading center, a listening center, a writing center, a discussion center, an art center, and a bookbinding center.

Reading Center.   The reading center should foster wide independent reading as materials of a variety of types and levels are available to students. The center should be an inviting place with attractive displays and comfortable chairs or

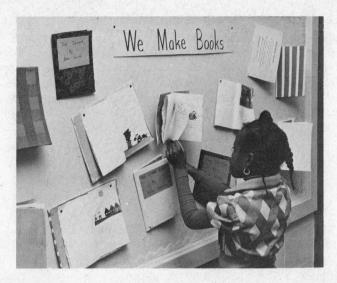

rugs. The children's literature materials in the center will lead to creative writing and other language experience activities. Pupil displays of art work and writing correlated with literature should be evident here. The reading center, too, is a place for displaying children's independent writing in the form of individual and class books. Children should participate in the arrangement of the center and can assume partial responsibility for the displays of their work. Many of the ideas suggested in chapters 3 and 4 can be used in the reading center.

Listening Center.   A listening center should include a tape recorder, record player, and sets of headphones and plug-in jacks. Teachers have found that tapes and records which can be used by children with little or no teacher direction can be extremely useful both for direct instruction and for independent learning. Children's literature selections can be taped and replayed by individuals or small groups. Children can record their creative stories. Motivation for meaningful oral reading can be provided as pupils tape materials for their classmates and for other classes and grades. As children find enjoyable passages in their independent reading, they can tape these. Teachers can play the tapes to evaluate pupils' oral reading skills.

For directed lessons with listening center materials, teachers can tape directions to correlate with a particular lesson and can have children follow directions from the tape without requiring the presence of the teacher. Certain phonics lessons are quite appropriate for taped presentation. Publishers now have a quantity of tapes and records to correlate with all content areas. Also popular for listening centers are "read-along" materials which include books so children can watch the print while hearing the story on the tape. Many teachers are making their own "read-along" materials using favorite literature selections and pupil-composed language experience stories.

Writing Center.   Another important center is the writing center which should serve as a stimulus for personal writing and for additional independent activities directly correlated with the language experience instruction. The writing center should include such essentials as commercial and class picture dictionaries, class word banks, pencils, crayons, paper, and the like. Pictures and objects can be placed in this center to stimulate creative writing. As in all centers, ideas will need to be changed frequently to maintain interest. The materials in the writing center can provide an excellent means for following-up previous language lessons or activities. For example, if a class is studying descriptive words, the teacher can reinforce this content by asking the children to write descriptive words for objects or pictures in the writing center or to write a story using descriptive words. The writing center should serve as an invitation to write, not as a required assignment for pupils.

Of course, at the very early stages of reading development, the activities in the writing center will need considerable structure, but as children grow in reading power, less help will be necessary. Beginning readers may wish to practice handwriting by copying a group experience story, but they should not be required to do this. In the very early stage of learning to read, model sentences can be used in the writing center with some element of word choice. For example, to provide practice in reading and writing color words, objects and pictures along with word cards for each object and picture can be placed in the writing center. The model sentence could be "A _____ is yellow," with pictures of pencils, paper, bananas, pears, the sun, and butter. Children could write a sentence, illustrate it, and use it for a group book. Other model sentence ideas might be "Round things" or "I like to _____," with pictures and phrases such as "ride my bike," "play football," "play with dolls," or "run in the leaves."

In chapter 4, the teaching of creative writing was discussed. A teacher can follow up the direct instruction in types and techniques of writing with examples in the writing center. For example, if a class were working on tall tales, the writing center could feature examples from both children's writings and literature. Pictures or topics for additional tall tales could be suggested as an independent activity. This use of the writing center could be adapted for each type and technique of writing.

A popular idea for a writing center is the use of pictures with questions and captions to stimulate writing. Some suggestions are:

Can you write an animal story?
Can you write an imaginary story?
Can you write a story about snow?
Can you make up a surprise ending for these pictures?
What descriptive words can you use to describe how the child in this picture felt?

The ideas for the writing center are inexhaustible since the illustrations, captions, and questions can be extremely varied.

Discussion Center. Stimuli for language experience stories can be placed in the discussion center for small groups to gather and discuss their ideas prior to writing and/or dictating stories. Appointing pupil leaders to conduct some discussions may lead to more involvement in oral language than when the teacher always serves as a discussion leader. The discussion center may make it possible for a teacher to offer additional oral language situations for some children who are minimally involved in large group discussions for language experience stories. Open-ended questions and situations can serve to stimulate creative and critical thinking. Examples of questions are "What do you think about . . . ?" "What would you do if . . . ?"

Art Center. Some teachers may not regard the art center as a part of the reading environment. However, in language experience reading programs art is an invaluable stimulus for creating through language. Art activities often lead to language involvement and language activities often lead to artistic expression. The language experience products which contain illustrations are usually far more appealing than those which do not, and the illustrations contribute to the pride in authorship which is so important in language experience learning. Literature experiences lead easily to interpretation through art. The displays recommended for the reading center offer an excellent way to incorporate art with the reading program.

Bookbinding Center. A helpful center in language experience classrooms is the bookbinding center which makes it possible for children to make attractive and durable products from their stories. Needed are cloth for covers, along with heavy cardboard, large needles, and thread. The booklet *Cover to Cover*[4] provides detailed, illustrated explanations of the steps in bookbinding. The following material is reprinted from *Cover to Cover.*[*]

Step 1
Stack the completed pages and add two extra pages, one before the title page and one after the final page.

Step 2
Fasten the pages together along the left edge or at the top, depending on the way the book is to open. Staples will be adequate for books of a few pages, but sewing is more durable. Sewing may be done by hand and can be done on a sewing machine using the longest stitch.

[4]*Cover to Cover* (Chicago: Encyclopaedia Britannica Press.) This is a free booklet.
[*]Reprinted by permission.

Step 3
Cut two pieces of cardboard
one-fourth inch larger in each
direction than the page size. If shirt
cardboard is used, a double thickness
may be desired.

Step 4
Tape the two pieces of cardboard
together with a one-fourth inch
separation between them so that the
cover is hinged.

Step 5
Place the cardboard on the cover
material and cut a piece large enough
to extend one full inch around the
outer edge of the cardboard.

Step 6
Remove the cardboard and coat the
reverse side of the cover material
with glue. An easy formula is 3 parts
Elmer's Glue and one part water.
This can be spread easily. Replace the
hinged cardboard and fold the edges
of the cover material around the
cardboard. Pull the cover edges
tightly to remove puckers and
bubbles.

Step 7
Cut a piece of colored construction
paper large enough to cover the
inside of the book cover and paste it
in place over the edges of the cover
material.

Step 8
Fasten the bound pages into the book
with tape. Construction paper the
same color as the inside of the cover
can be cut and pasted in place to
cover the tape.

Evaluation in the Language Experience Approach

Evaluation is a continuous process and is a part of all curriculum experiences. Informal evaluation will occur in everyday situations with spoken and written language. More formal evaluation will come in the form of record keeping and standardized testing.

The checklists suggested in chapter 8 are also part of the evaluation. Self-evaluation is encouraged as children note the increase in the amount of vocabulary in their word banks, as they keep folders of their written stories, and as they discuss their progress with the teacher. The pride in authorship should lead to positive evaluation. Stauffer relates an incident of a first grade child rereading at the end of a school year the stories composed in November. The child's comment was, "That's the way I wrote when I was little."[5]

In the language experience approach, the teacher must evaluate children's learning in reading and the other language arts in terms of the instructional goals discussed in chapter 2. Those goals can be stated in question form as guides for teacher evaluation of reading and language programs: Are children growing in their ability to use reading as a medium of communication? Are their reading vocabularies increasing? Are they developing favorable attitudes and genuine interest in reading? Are they using effective strategies to unlock unfamiliar words? Questions related to communication through language should also be asked in regard to the goal statements of Smith[6] and Applegate[7] found in chapter 2. The teacher should ask, too, whether children are responding creatively in the language experience activities.

Final Summary

Teaching reading as a language experience rests on a philosophy of personal, communicative, creative, and functional learning and teaching. Instruction is built on children's existing level of language expression as speech is encoded with written symbols and as they read the written record of their spoken thoughts.

Language study in speaking, listening, reading, and writing occurs in situations which contain and stimulate a high degree of pupil involvement. Pupil-developed materials are central to instruction in the language experience framework. The language experience approach is used as a bridge from pre-reading to beginning reading, as a component of a balanced reading program in combination with other approaches, as a means of reaching the discouraged remedial reader and the adult illiterate, and as a means of providing materials relevant to disadvantaged children.

---

[5]Russell G. Stauffer, *The Language Experience Approach to the Teaching of Reading* (New York: Harper and Row, Publishers, 1970), p. 107.

[6]James A. Smith, *Adventures in Communication* (Boston: Allyn and Bacon, 1972), pp. 91–93.

[7]Mauree Applegate, *Easy in English* (Evanston, Ill.: Row, Peterson and Company, 1960), p. 8.

The instructional program stresses creative writing, vocabulary development, and literary experiences in a classroom based on flexibility, receptiveness, and stimulation. The classroom setting includes learning centers where children can pursue independent language activities. Individual, small group, and total group instruction are included in the language experiences. As teachers evaluate the children's ability to communicate through spoken and written language, they base their evaluation on the goals of reading and language instruction.

Suggested Readings

Allen, R. Van. *Language Experiences in Reading*. Chicago: Encyclopaedia Britannica Press, 1974. In the manuals for language experience programs in these materials, Allen describes the use of centers as part of the ongoing language experience classroom.

Waynant, Louise F., and Wilson, Robert M. *Learning Centers . . . A Guide For Effective Use*. Paoli, Pa.: The Instructo Corporation, 1974. Teachers who wish specific guidelines for implementing learning centers will find this reference particularly helpful.

Index